D1417258

LET THE HAMMER DOWN!

LET THE HAMMER DOWN!

JERRY CLOWER

with Gerry Wood

WORD BOOKS
PUBLISHER
4800 WEST WACO DRIVE
WACO, TEXAS
76703

LET THE HAMMER DOWN!
by Jerry Clower with Gerry Wood
Copyright © 1978 by Jerry Clower

ISBN 0-8499-0062

Library of Congress catalog card number: 77-92448

Printed in the United States of America

Contents

Introduction

By GERRY WOOD

Hello, again, Jay-ree!

I'm writing this by candlelight. No, I haven't forsaken electricity. Electricity has forsaken me.

One of our rip-roaring Tennessee thunderstorms has zapped the Franklin, Tennessee, power lines, leaving not only me in the dark, but, somewhere across Franklin, leaving your manager Tandy Rice in the dark.

Which is one of the few times you'll ever find both of us in the dark.

A lot of water has gone over the dam since we put *The End* on our first book. You've continued to travel the country, becoming an even bigger national star.

The week that *Ain't God Good!* came out was the most remarkable week of my life. Not only did the new book hit the stands, but, in the same week, I got a new car, a new home, and a new job. Plus plenty of offers to do more books.

And I've been doing my share of traveling, too, trying to make Amtrak profitable by riding the Panama Limited, Floridian, Inter-American and San Francisco Zephyr. Making my first trip to Europe, I also rode the Orient Express.

Move over, Paul Theroux, there's another railroad buff/writer chugging right behind you!

The reaction to the first book was incredible. The reviews sounded as though our mothers had written them. The book was read on ships in the Pacific, atop fire towers in the woods, on planes and trains, and in the comfort of living room couches and the privacy of bathtubs.

I'd like to say thanks to my folks, Gladys and Albert Wood, who got me here. My Uncle Leon, who published a book of inspirational poetry while in his 80s, and inspires me here. My late Auntie Dora whose torch for living I carry. My wife Ellen who keeps me here, and whose major efforts are reflected on the pages of this book. And my friends who put up with me.

So now we're ready for more of your hilarious tales of the South, your philosophy that never lets a complicated word or thought get between you and the truth, your passion for living and capacity for loving.

One of my favorite writers, E. B. White, once said, "I'd rather watch a gifted plumber than listen to a bad poet."

Tell us about those gifted plumbers, those artists-at-living. Those folks not only know how to let the hammer down, they know what kind of ammunition to use.

Let it down, Brother Jerry, and we'll have another good book.

LET THE HAMMER DOWN!

I

Let the Hammer Down!

Back when I lived in Brookhaven, Mississippi, years ago, Lance Alworth was in high school. I got to see him play each and every high school game he participated in.

He was an artist on the football field. He later went on to be an all-American at Arkansas and all-pro wide receiver. And that high school team was a fantastic team coached by Paul Moyer.

Up in the stands, a gentleman had a yell he used to do. He'd cup his hands to his mouth and yell, "Let the hammer down!"

Well, I picked that up. When I moved on to Yazoo City, Mississippi, I'd yell at the Yazoo City Indians, "Let the hammer down!"

One evening at a football game, Mrs. Lucile Barbour turned around and looked up at me. She's a very fine lady with way above average means and from one of the most prominent families in Mississippi.

"Mr. Clower, what do you mean when you yell at our young men, 'Let the hammer down!'?"

"Mrs. Barbour, have you ever seen one of them long-tong shotguns? A 32-inch barrel, full choke, that had a hammer on it, and you took your thumb and thumb-cocked it?"

"Oh, yes, my father had one of those."

"Well, if your father had that gun pointed at something and it was loaded, and he let the hammer down, it was effective, wasn't it?"

"It sure was."

The message sunk in.

So folks around me at the football games started yelling, "Let the hammer down!"

To me, that's saying, "Do the best you can with what you've got—and do it now."

All my life, I've had a genuine zest for living. I've never tried to be anything but myself. So in this book I'm recommending that each and every individual have a genuine zest for living. Never appear to be anything but yourself, and do it with maximum effort. And I'll call this—*Let the Hammer Down!*

Now, we've already written a book called *Ain't God Good!* It started off on September 28, 1926, on a dirt road at Route 4, Liberty, Mississippi. This one is starting off by me being in show business and still having a genuine zest for living. And I never appear to be anything but myself. And, my, how happy I am and how happy others can be by doing this, and by saying, "Let the hammer down!"

Living Ain't Nothing But Fun. I thought about that for the title of this book. It makes a lot of sense.

Folks, those of you reading this book, I'm sure when you saw the title, *Let the Hammer Down!*, you assumed it was about CB radios. "Let the Hammer Down" was a favorite expression of mine, and I've been yelling it before CB radios were ever invented. This in no way has anything to do with that now popular saying, "Let the hammer down," while you talk on CB radios, but it applies just as well.

Whatever you do, do it good, and do it with maximum effort. Then you, too, will be *letting the hammer down.*

This is
Gerry Wood.

My wife, Homerline, the glue what holds me together

Me and my grandson, Jayree. Guess where he got his name

This is Katy, my baby . . . the one
what sneaked up on me and mama.

Me and Chief Hill shot this honker in Reelfoot Lake, Tennessee

Another look at grandson Jayree

With Gov. Cliff Finch of Mississippi at a press conference

L. to R.: Katy, Homerline, Sue, me and grandson Jayree

One of my closest friends is Muttering Mel Tillis. Here we are doing dog chow commercials together.

Me with Jim Rupe's daughters. He's my favorite pilot.

L. to R.: Bishop John Allin, Congressman Sonny Montgomery, me, and my manager, Tandy Rice

Wendy Holcomb and Jim Ed Brown, who host my weekly TV show, "Nashville on the Road," with me. *Dev O'Neill photo.*

2

Cold Nights and Hot Hotels

Here I am in show business, Jerry Clower, a former fertilizer salesman. And that first book I wrote, *Ain't God Good!*, good gracious alive!, Pocket Books has bought the paperback rights to that thing and now it's on every newsstand in America for $1.75.

I've been knowing for a long time that I have a lot of fans, and they love me. But I want to hasten to say I have a lot more fans who love me a $1.75 worth than they do $6.95! The book sold more than 500,000 copies in paperback in the first two months it was released, and it's still selling.

However, the book sold real good at $6.95 in the hardback. And Word, my publisher asked me to do another one, so I contacted my co-writer Mr. Gerry Wood, and he said, "Jerry, let's let the hammer down!"

So here I am writing another book. Right in the middle of show business. I just came off a tour to promote the paperback of *Ain't God Good!*, the book I wrote first.

23

LET THE HAMMER DOWN!

The tour started off Monday, January 3, in Boston. Wheew, just think of that! Good gracious, I get to Boston at the airport and it's zero degrees outside, but a hundred degrees inside.

Why they keep the airports and hotels in the Northern cities so hot, I'll never be able to understand. I turned off every thermostat in my room and still like to have suffocated. I raised the window a little bit and that helped. But then you could hear the sirens blowing on the police cars outside, and I couldn't rest.

But I still had a great visit in Boston. On this tour, gracious alive, a television interview at 8:15 the next morning. At 11, a press interview. At 12, a press interview and at 1 p.m. a radio interview. At 5 p.m., depart Boston and go to New York City. And spend all day in New York City.

A fine, pretty hotel, but it's still too cotton pickin' hot. There ought to be a law passed that it's a criminal offense if they get those hotels over 70 degrees.

What a great time I had. I've never had such a beautiful time as promoting this paperback book *Ain't God Good!* and traveling on this tour.

Monday I spent all day in Boston. Tuesday all day in New York, Wednesday in Little Rock, Thursday all day in Dallas–Ft. Worth, Friday all day in Houston and San Antonio, Sunday in Abilene, Tex., and Los Angeles, Tuesday morning in Los Angeles, and then I caught a big jet to Des Moines.

It was 7 degrees below zero. Wheew! The hotel there was too hot, but you had each individual room controlling the temperature. That's what I like. I turned it slap off and it took about eight hours for it to get cool enough for me. Then I eased the thermostat back up and I was comfortable. I slept so good in Des Moines, Iowa.

This was Tuesday when I flew into Des Moines to

do a show. Then, early the next morning, I flew to Minneapolis. Haaaw! Twenty-eight degrees *below* zero! I slept *between* the mattresses in the bed up there. I was scared to death that everybody was just going to freeze to death while I was there.

On Thursday, I spent all day in Chicago, then Friday all day in Atlanta. Friday night I caught that jet to Jackson, Mississippi, got in my Dodge pickup truck and drove home to mama.

One of the reasons I want to say something about this tour is because it was just fantastic. See, I've been spoiled. I worked for a very good company, the Mississippi Chemical Corporation, before I backed into show business—and that company does things right.

The department I headed sold over a hundred million dollars worth of plant food annually. And if the salesman told me he would meet me at eight o'clock, our meeting took place at eight o'clock. If I told a salesman I'd meet him at six o'clock, I met him at six o'clock. You weren't ever in doubt whether somebody was going to show up or not and mess you up.

Inasmuch as I now work with Top Billing Inc. in Nashville, and Mr. Tandy Rice of that company is my manager, and they do things right, decently and in order, I just knew when I went on this tour for Pocket Books that they wouldn't know what they were doing.

But they did.

My soul, everything was right on time. And I had such a great time going on the tour.

The reason the tour was so successful is because Pocket Books took enough trouble to plan the schedule and then they executed the schedule and it ultimately resulted in . . . *letting the hammer down!*

3

Me and Marcel

Anything I say or any illustration I give about my Christian convictions or anything about the Lord is facts. I may, however, embellish a little bit on a story. But, in all of the stories I tell, something happened to give me the inspiration to tell it.

I'd like to say that I took Marcel Ledbetter with me on this big tour when I went up to Boston. We got in that hot hotel and he started complaining.

"Jerry, I ain't gonna sleep this hot."

"Marcel, come on with me, son, and let's go down to the dining room and I'll buy you a real good supper."

We walked into the dining room and the maitre d' came up. "Oh, Mr. Clower, I recognize you from having seen you on television on your 'Nashville on the Road' show. And I've seen you doing the Dodge pickup truck commercials and selling Purina Dog Chow on television. Come right over here and have a seat."

Me and Marcel Ledbetter ate some of that fine food in that plush restaurant. The maitre d' had said, "Welcome to the land of the bean and the cod." So we ate us some of that fish that's world famous up there in Boston. It was a good meal.

We got through eating and walked up to the cash register. A good-looking lady was sitting up on a tall stool and had gold chains around her neck, diamonds on her fingers, and she even smelled good.

While I was paying the check, Marcel reached over in a bowl of loose toothpicks, got him one, and commenced to picking his teeth. He was picking 'em good.

The lady stared at Marcel. And Marcel put the toothpick back over in the bowl, looked at her, and said, "Lady, I'll bet you a lot of folks use them toothpicks and walk off with 'em."

The next morning I sent Marcel Ledbetter home.

I ain't trying to rehabilitate Marcel. I love him the way he is. If he asks my opinion on some of the things he does, I try to counsel with him.

One day when I was going to school I was walking to the old country schoolhouse. I was about to be late, and I met Marcel coming back. "Marcel, why are you leaving school?"

"Ain't no need to go to school today. Somebody let the air out of the basketball."

So we both went on to the house.

Back about that same time, Marcel's uncle died. Uncle Looney Douglas. His wife was Aunt Penny.

Me and Marcel had to go to the funeral and we were sitting by Aunt Penny. Uncle Looney Douglas was up there in the casket.

As the preacher got up to start the service, Aunt Penny started squalling. "Looney, speak to me! Looney, please, raise up, darling. Say something to me!"

Marcel said, "Aunt Penny, if he does, that window's mine."

That Marcel is something else. He told me recently that he has found a cure for baldness.

"I've done figured me out a way to put hair up on top of their head."

"Marcel, how do you do that?"

"Well, I get me a quart of alum juice and a quart of green persimmon juice. I mix it together half and half. They'll massage the top of their head with that concoction."

"Will it grow hair on their head?"

"No, but it'll draw their sideburns up on top of their head."

One day Marcel came walking to school about 11 o'clock in the morning.

The teacher ran out and said, "What in the world are you doing coming this late to school?"

Marcel kind of ducked his head. "Prof Turner, there's been some weasels or foxes or something getting papa's chickens. Papa had been trying to catch that thing in the henhouse. This morning about four o'clock in the morning, before daylight, we heard them chickens holler.

"Papa said, 'Marcel, get up, son, we're fixing to kill that thing what's getting our chickens.' Papa got up and loaded that thirty-two inch double-barrel shotgun. Put

29

that big load in there, thumb-cocked that thing. And starts easing around the side of the house, creeping along with me. He had that shotgun pointed right at the chickenhouse.

"Papa sleeps in a nightgown. Nothing else. And just as we walked up to that chickenhouse, papa with his hand on that trigger, saying, 'Shhh, we're fixing to get this thing now, Marcel,' my best coondog, old Brumey, eased up behind papa and coldnosed him up under that gown. BOOOM!

"The reason I'm late to school is that I've been picking chickens ever since."

4

Lust and Money

Some very interesting things happened on the tour for Pocket Books. Several times I had the opportunity to let the hammer down.

One of the things that really impressed me is how a man like me is interviewed on some stations.

With the new president being the only president in the White House without an accent, a lot of people want to ask me about that. On KHJ television in Los Angeles, they brought me on by showing a film clip of the old Ma and Pa Kettle movies while John Denver was singing "Country Boy." They brought me on as a good old boy, we had a beautiful interview and a good time, and I thoroughly enjoyed the hospitality of this very fine TV station.

The co-hosts of this morning show were George Putnam and Tom Hawkins.

But when it came time for a break, George said, "We'll be back in a minute, and we're going to ask

Jerry Clower, the Christian entertainer, something about how much money is made off religion these days, and if he has ever lusted after women. We'll be right back."

When we came back, George looked at me and asked, "Jerry, have you ever lusted after women?"

My answer to that was, "Any red-blooded American human being that is of the male species in this old world who says he has never looked at an attractive lady and didn't get ideas in his head is telling a bald-faced lie. But, hallelujah, God never intended for us to have a craving flung on us that he didn't also outline a way for that craving to be satisfied—decently, romantically, and beautifully.

"You see, when I see an attractive lady and she, in fact, throws a craving on me, it simply thrills me to know I'm going home to mama. Now that's the way it ought to be done. That's the way God said to do it. It's not a sin to be tempted, but it is a sin to yield to your temptations. So when I see an attractive lady, it just reminds me of how soon I hope the tour is over and I can get on home to see mama, the lady I have been seeing for thirty years."

"Jerry, what about all this money that's being made off religion?"

I looked him in the eye and said, "Sir, I happen to be a Christian and I belong to a Southern Baptist church. And we don't own no stock exchanges and we don't do no farming on a large scale to make money. The Southern Baptist church preaches that you ought to give to our almighty God because we love Him.

"We also suggest a minimum of a tithe. So I tithe my income to the First Baptist Church of Yazoo City, Mississippi. And I advocate strongly that all assets owned by a church ought to be taxed except the building they worship in. Personally, I wouldn't object too much if taxes had to be paid on that, too. Now, let me make sure that there's no misunderstanding here, sir."

The host was astonished. "Are you serious?"

"I'm as serious as I've ever been in my life. I believe all church property, all church functions, all church activities ought to be taxed with the exception of the building they worship in.

"Back when I was selling fertilizer, the largest farms I called on were owned by a church. Now, something has got to give. There is a lot of money made off religion, but there's not too much money cleared off Christianity except money that goes to the glory of God. You know, at my church we don't have any cake walks and stuff like that to raise money. We preach that folks ought to give money because they love God and because God loves us first."

Praise God, I was an active enough Christian and had studied the Bible enough to know how to give him an answer on television to that question.

That answer could be classified as letting the hammer down.

I don't intend to criticize any group here that takes advantage of the laws. I blame the United States Congress for letting this go on. It's just got out of hand.

Here is a clandestine group of folks. They don't know any more about living a Christian life than a billy goat. They have big promotions and holler and whoop and do big deals, and it's a nonprofit thing, but three or four folks are getting rich and they pay no taxes.

So, any good organization or group that's doing something worthwhile and complying with the laws of the land, it's not my intention to be critical of them here in this book—not one little bit. But I'm saying the United States Congress ought to pass a law that all of these functions will be taxed and that will cut out some of this, and we can get it on and have more money to run the government.

5

Route 4 Roots

I grew up at Route 4, Liberty, Mississippi.

If you want to know where that is, the Mainline of Mid-America—the Illinois Central Railroad—runs from Chicago down to New Orleans. That big train, the Panama Limited, runs on it. That was the greatest thing on wheels when I was a young'un growing up. They sleep on there.

I saw a big car the other day that had "Limited" on the side of it. I went and bought it. If it had had "Panama" on the front of it, I would have bought two.

If you want to know where I grew up, go to that railroad. Whatever side of the railroad you live on, you head out toward it and go to McComb, Mississippi, then go twelve miles west of McComb, straight out in the woods, and slam on brakes, and you'll be in downtown East Fork, Mississippi.

That's where I first saw the light of day.

Every Saturday night we would listen to the Grand Ole Opry. The only thing we had to entertain ourselves was a battery radio. The battery was dead on it most of the time.

We found out you could set that battery down in front of the fireplace and run and plug it in while it was hot, and it'd play as long as the battery stayed hot.

LET THE HAMMER DOWN!

Every Saturday night we'd go to whoever's house in the community had the strongest battery on the radio. We'd tune it in to one of those big country stations. We'd tune it up loud and hear that beautiful music. We'd get the volume up high and snatch the knobs off the radio so nobody could move it off that station.

East Fork community of Amite County, Mississippi, had a country store that I refer to in my albums and books as being run by Mr. Duvall Scott. It was where all the schoolbus drivers hung out. He was a fine old man.

He never rang up the cash register unless he quoted something from the Bible. He was that religious. His young'uns were named Matthew, Mark, Luke, and John . . . and Ebenezer. He quoted the Bible about everything.

These schoolbus drivers would sit back in the rear of this old country store playing dominoes. And they'd watch Mr. Duvall Scott. Everytime a sale was made, they'd be interested to know what kind of Scripture verse he was going to recite.

One morning when it was raining, a little child came in and bought a penny's worth of candy. Mr. Duvall Scott mashed the cash register and said, "Suffer the little children. Come unto me."

Soon another customer came in. It was a man who wanted to buy something for his daddy. He bought the gift, and as he left, Mr. Duvall Scott hit the cash register and said, "Honor thy father and mother."

About that time a big van stopped out front. It was being pulled by a long, fancy, rich car. The man wanted to buy a blanket for a horse.

"Yeah, I got a horse blanket." Mr. Duvall Scott went back and got one off the shelf. "That'll be five dollars."

"You don't understand. I'm on my way to a big horse show down in Louisiana. This here is an expensive horse. I don't put five dollar blankets on him."

"Wait just a minute, I'll check and see what else I've

got." He went back, but he didn't have but one kind. All of them were the same. He reached up there and got a different color. He brought it out. "This'll be twenty-five dollars."

"Man, I wouldn't put a twenty-five dollar blanket on a world-renowned horse. Ain't you got something better than this?"

"Well, I got one more. Let me go back and see." He went back to the same pile, got a different color, and flopped it down, saying, "That'll be fifty dollars."

"That's more like it."

The customer paid the fifty dollars, covered up his horse, and drove off. And there were all of those school bus drivers sitting back there staring at Mr. Duvall Scott.

He rang that cash register, looked toward the heavens, moved his lips a little bit, and said, "He was a stranger and I took him in."

Some of my favorite stories are about people who think they're fooling somebody else only to discover that the shoe is on the other foot.

One year New-Gene Ledbetter went off on a big 4-H Club Roundup up in Chicago. He told his papa, Uncle Virsi, that he had to take things to swap with some of the other boys coming in from states all over the country.

Some of those Yankee 4-H Clubs boys were making fun of those Southern farm boys. But when New-Gene came back, he had $387, all in one dollar bills.

Uncle Virsi got a dried brush broom. "New-Gene, you done robbed the bank."

"I ain't no such, poppa. I ain't done nothing wrong. I just took advantage of some ignorant people. I can't help it if they're crazy."

"Well, how did you get this money?"

37

"Daddy, I took a big sack of cockleburs with me. I sold them to them Yankee boys for a dollar apiece as porcupine eggs."

When I was a young'un growing up, there was a big counterfeit ring up North out of St. Louis, Missouri. One of their big engraving machines went haywire and printed a bunch of fifteen dollar bills.

The bad guys said, "What're we gonna do with all these fifteen dollar bills?"

"I'll tell you what we'll do," one of them said. "We'll go down to Mississippi where they're kind of dumb. We'll go to some of those country stores and get them changed, and bring good money back to St. Louis."

They came down through Highway 24 into Liberty, Mississippi, and saw Mr. Duvall Scott's store.

"Sir, do you run this store?" they asked.

"I do."

"I got a fifteen dollar bill here I'd like to get changed."

"Beautiful, I'd be glad to do it for you." He rang the cash register. "How would you like it? Do you want two sixes and a three? Or three threes and a six? Or would you rather have five three dollar bills?"

One hot July day me and Marcel were sitting at the country store when this big, long car stopped. A fancy dude from the city got out, walked up, and said, "Hey, country boy. That's about a sixty pound watermelon right there. I'll give you five dollars if you can eat it."

"I believe I can eat that watermelon," Marcel said. "But let me run up to the house just for a minute and I'll be right back and let you know whether I can eat it or not."

Marcel was gone for a few minutes. When he came back, he said, "Yes, sir!"

And he busted that melon, ate every bit of it, scraped the rind, drank the juice, sucked it up out of there, jumped up and said, "Give me my five dollars."

"You sure did eat all of that watermelon. I've got your five dollars, but before I give it to you, why did you have to run up to the house before you'd know whether you could eat this watermelon or not?"

"Papa's got one up there at the house under the bed about the same size as this one. I knowed if I could eat that one, I could eat this one."

When the draft got after Marcel, he wanted to be in the Navy. The Army was about to draft him, and he wanted to figure out a way to where he wouldn't pass for the Army so he could join the Navy.

So he went to the recruiting sergeant at McComb, Mississippi, walked in and said, "I've come to join the Army."

"Fine. Sit down and let's fill out some forms."

"I ain't got time to fill out no forms. I want to get a'holt of them now. I want you to fly me nonstop to the South Sea Islands. I want to invade one of them islands. I want to crawl on my belly at Iwo Jima and grab one of them in the throat hand-to-hand. I want to take a knife and *stawb* one of them! I want to dig a tunnel up under one of them bunkers and come up and throw one of them hand grenades. Hawwwwwchh! And holler Gung Ho! I want to choke them. I want hand-to-hand combat, to grab them by the hair of the head, jump out of palm trees, and swim under the water. I want to eyeball the baddest one over there and whup up on him. I'm ready to go now. I don't want no training!"

The sergeant jumped up. "Fellow, you're crazy."

Marcell said, "Write that down."

6

Behind the Scenes

People come up to me all over the country and say, "Jerry, boy, are you something else! We think you're a tremendous fellow. Your TV show 'Nashville on the Road.' . . . You do such a beautiful job. Those Purina Dog Food commercials, especially the ones you and Mel Tillis did together—man, you something."

I hear this everywhere. Then they'll say, "The year you were the spokesman for Dodge pickup trucks all over the nation. . . ."

And I got to thinking, it's high time that credit goes to those who drag those cables, those who stay up all night getting the set ready for the next day, those among us who are technicians and can really do the sound good, those among us who can really know how to point that camera, those among us who can paint the sets, who can set up this stuff.

I'd like to reproduce portions of an inter-office memorandum that was sent out three days before we were to do a Dodge pickup truck commercial at Jefferson Pilot Broadcasting in Charlotte, N.C.

Everybody runs up to me and says, "Jerry, how great you are." But, look, my, what a great group of people are behind the scenes. It's unbelievable.

The average layman probably wouldn't fathom what's involved in doing a commercial. I'd like to pay tribute to those people who are behind the scenes, who do all the work, but folks like Jerry Clower get all the credit.

This memorandum is dated Monday, April 23, and there are thirteen people who get a copy of this memo from the big boss. It's a great big memorandum—two pages. And this is something!

Interoffice Correspondence—Jefferson Pilot Broadcasting

To:	Those Listed	V. Torrence	C. Whitney
		E. Wade	M. Johnson
From:	George Booker	J. Wilson	B. Dycus (5)
		D. McDaniel	K. Helms
Date:	April 23, 1976	S. Triebwasser	Jan Thompson
		B. Buckner	R. Bailey
		T. Singleton	

Re: Schedule/Crews Wk April 26th

Note the following schedule information—and lack of information—regarding Dodge M–T–W of next week and also the O'Herron For Governor xsfer and edit on Tuesday with the Film Department.

Monday, April 23rd and Tuesday, April 24th:
Two days with the one camera unit for BBD&O (Pete Barnes)—Dodge Trucks.
On Monday we will shoot at a lake site up on Lake Norman; that site location to be determined today with the Director, Dick Willis. We will also set the call later today

42

when the Client and Director get in; probably an early call in the vicinity of 6:30 or 7:00 am; will advise.

The crew for Monday's shoot as follows:

Director: Dick Willis
CDL/Notes: Marion Johnson
Make-up: Jan Thompson
Cameraman: Jerry Wilson
Crew: McDaniel, Torrence, Triebwasser, Buckner

We will take several vehicles to this site: a Winnebago for the Client, GMC w/90 and 3000, two Dodge 'props' (maroon van/red and white fancy pick-up),* transportation for the trip up.

The Winnebago will be 'stocked' for Client use; we will also have drinks in it (soft drinks!) for the crew. Marion will be in charge of the Winnebago supplies and also lunch on location. Where we get lunch and how shooting on the lake we will determine with Marion this afternoon when the site is picked.

The gaffers truck is being loaded this morning per a long list put together by Jerry. All trucks are being gassed this morning for the trip. Keys to each vehicle will be passed out this afternoon.

The above crew holds for Monday and Tuesday with one exception: Stu Triebwasser will not work the Dodge shoot on location Tuesday. Stu will work the JP Studio full day edit of O'Herron For Governor . . . cards and projection.

Tuesday's Dodge shoot will be a farm location somewhere out Providence Road in the near vicinity to Highway 51.

*(Note: I'm wrong here—it's the blue and silver short bed truck on Monday with the maroon van . . . not the red and white pick-up, which works Tuesday).

LET THE HAMMER DOWN!

This location will be set later today and also the fax time and call for this day.

The crew for this day the same as Monday with the exception of Stu as noted.

Our vehicles this day will consist of the Winnebago, GMC, Dodge gaffers with the generator and Dodge vehicles: red & white fancy pick-up, red-stripped pick-up (from Monroe), lite gold/parchment from Freedom Dodge, baby-blue pick-up with camper on back. We will also have as props: plumbing pipes, tools, etc., for one truck, fertilizer, hay, fork, etc., for another vehicle; supplies for camper for family going on a trip to the beach (folding chairs, etc.).

Wednesday, April 28th:
This is the edit day for BBD&O/Dodge. Call is 8:30 am.

Director:	Dick Willis
TD:	Jerry Wilson
CDL:	Marion Johnson
Studio:	One man (TBD)

cc: Hodges
     Upchurch
     Pressley
     McCorkle
     File

Now I have a dressing room and there's a lady who follows me around, and every time a drop of sweat comes out on my head, she dobs it off. It's just unbelievable the amount of work that goes into doing a commercial.
So I want to pay homage and give tribute right here to all of these people at these ad agencies and broadcast studios that make commercials. What a great job they do!

When you see a commercial, it isn't just the guy standing there. He probably does less work than anybody on the set. I want to pay tribute to these unsung heroes.

Also, people run up to me and say, "Oh, Jerry, I heard you on the Grand Ole Opry. Man, ain't you something. Good gracious alive, the Grand Ole Opry!"

Or they'll say, "Jerry, I heard you on the Opry and you sounded good."

I wish there was some way they would know right off that a man named Uncle Dave Macon back in 1925 started performing and, thus, the Grand Ole Opry was born. And millions of dollars, bricks, mortar, and fantastically talented human beings make the world-famous Grand Ole Opry what it is.

Cold chills run up and down my spine every time I do a show on the Opry because I stand on some boards under my feet that Hank Williams stood on, Red Foley stood on, and so many other country music greats stood on.

To be able to perform now with internationally known people like Roy Acuff and Minnie Pearl and many, many others is a fantastic delight for me.

One of the highlights of my life was when I was inducted into the Grand Ole Opry in 1973. Some of the stars that perform there are some of the greatest talents in the world. But, my, what powerful people are behind it all! What planning! What risks on putting up investment money to make the Grand Ole Opry how great it is today!

I'll always express my undying gratitude to those early pioneers who put the money on the line to buy the stock to start National Life & Accident Insurance Co. How successful they've been!

They were a bunch of folks that banded themselves together, believed in something, and let the hammer down. They had a dream and they worked that dream to perfection. In letting the hammer down, they let it down properly, decently, and in order. That's why there is a world-famous Grand Ole Opry.

Rather than hearing people say, "We heard you on the Opry and you did a good job," I'd get a lot bigger thrill if they said, "Ain't that a fantastic organization? Good gracious, isn't it wonderful that a group of people had enough faith to build it and make it, and now you have an opportunity to be a part of it?"

On the set of a recent "Almost Anything Goes"
TV taping in Atlanta

Sandy Brokaw handles PR for me in
Los Angeles. He's a hoss!

Me and some of my fans! *Robert Jackson photo.*

My first appearance on the Grand Ole Opry is a memory I'll cherish . . . *Bert Tippett photo.*

I collect hats everywhere I go. Here are some of my favorites.

Here's another
hat I enjoy
wearing.

Me and some of my mementoes

YARN SPINNER FROM YAZOO CITY

JERRY CLOWER

A devoted husband and father, Jerry is an enormous ex-varsity football lineman whose heart is as big as his physical frame. He has been very much in demand as a lay preacher and an after-dinner speaker in Mississippi and adjoining states for more than 16 years. He is employed at Mississippi Chemical Corp.

Clower, a leader among the Gideons, is a lay preacher and deacon in the First Baptist Church of Yazoo City...

One of the Recording Industry's coming stars. His homespun stories smack of the area, in South Mississippi where he grew up. He claims they're 90% true.

Jerry played in the first college football game he ever saw. A formidable opponent, he weighted in at 214 lbs and was 6 feet tall!

BILL DUKE-72

In Appreciation—The Nashville Banner Principal Speaker 1971 Banquet of Champions

Me and Ol' Ern. *Dana Pembroke Thomas photo.*

Me and Dennis Weaver. *Les Leverett photo.*

With Grant Teaff, Coach of the Baylor Bears. *Chris Hansen photo.*

David Frost is one of the best interviewers I know.

This beautiful man typifies
the fans who keep me going

These guys look just like
Marcel Ledbetter. They were m
hosts on a recent trip to Georgi

Two giants of the entertainment world:
Jarrell McCracken,   Mike Maitland, president of
president of Word Records   MCA Records

7

Coaches and the Headless Man

A dear friend of mine is very busy and doesn't read as much as he'd like to read. He buys Reader's Digest condensed books.

One day he was reading the Reader's Digest condensed book on the great men of our nation. My friend looked over at his wife and said, "Honey, you know there's not really as many great men in this world as you'd think." His wife looked at him and said, "I'm sure there may be one less than you think."

I live by a quotation that hangs in my office: "There is no limit to what can be done if it doesn't matter who gets the credit."

By expressing myself here, saying that other people ought to be recognized, I'm not denouncing that statement. I believe in it from the bottom of my heart.

What I'm saying is, we should make sure we understand why some things happen. Occasionally, we should give recognition to those who have meant so much to us.

LET THE HAMMER DOWN!

If you mentioned the name Bear Bryant, there are very few people in the world who wouldn't know who he is. Or who Darrell Royal is. Or Bud Wilkinson. Or Don Shula.

But what if I said the name, Red Jenkins? Have you ever heard of him? What about Sammy Howard, Peter Boston, Jerry Brown, Charlie Myers? Have you ever heard of them?

Well, they're a few high school coaches that have made a direct impact on my life because they coached my son in high school.

I'm not knocking the high calling of a college coach, and I love the contribution they make. But on occasion, I wish the national network TV announcer would say, "That young man who just made the beautiful run played with such-and-such high school and his coach was coach so-and-so."

High school football coaches in America collectively do more before breakfast for the masses of young men than all the college coaches will do for the rest of their lives. I'm serious when I say this.

The high school coach gets the boy who can't run. He gets the boy whose mama wants to come down to the high school to jump on the coach because her son doesn't start every game. He also fought the battle of court-ordered integration.

Friends, a lot of high schools, public schools worked because fine, dedicated high school coaches stayed and tried to make it work. Where you had a good athletic program, it was something to rally around.

It happened all over my native state, wherever they had a good sports program. It took a lot of pressure off the court-ordered integration.

The United States Congress should declare a National High School Coaches Week. And at least get Mr. Howard Cosell or Mr. Keith Jackson to occasionally say what an outstanding, great job high school coaches do in this country.

College coaches are great and I'm not knocking them. . . . A lot of them are my friends. But they just get the cream of the crop. They cull 'em down. They get the ones who can run the fastest. They just get the ones who can excel at what they do. But in high school, they worry with every kind that you can possibly come up with. They do a fantastic job.

Like I was saying about people who walk up to me and tell me that I did a wonderful job on a commercial, I wish they'd think a little bit about all the laborers who worked hard to make that commercial. And when they tell me I did a good job on the Opry, I hope the next thought is . . . *Man, didn't a bunch of folks do a good job making that Grand Ole Opry what it is!* Those people behind the scenes, some of us have never heard of. The same goes for the high school coaches. People say, "Man, look at that great college coach."

Think about the high school coach who took that boy when he was a little ole young'un, really molded him, and made him into something before that college coach ever got him.

Do the college coaches get mad about my views concerning high school coaches? Let me tell you a true story about what happened when I made these same comments at the Nashville *Banner* Banquet of Champions.

After I finished saying I wished high school coaches would be given more recognition, Vince Dooley, the coach of Georgia—the Southeastern Conference champions—came up to me and put his hand on my shoulder. He was very emotional. He looked me right in the eye and said a beautiful thing that proves what I'm saying here.

"Jerry, thank God you said what you did about high

school coaches. You see, me and my brother Bill, who coaches at the University of North Carolina, are always counseling with our high school coach. Seldom a week ever passes that we don't call our old high school coach and counsel with him, even now."

Now, friends, who can say the name of the high school coach who coached Vince Dooley and Bill Dooley? Has anybody ever heard of him? Do you know who he is? He's done more for young men at that high school post than some great college coach will do the rest of his life. His name is Ray Dicharry.

If we're not careful, we can look at the present and never think about the past that made the present possible. Back when I was a boy growing up, we used to think some things and know they were so, but find out later that what we thought wasn't true at all. Not near about true.

If there were a few hours of daylight left after we got the chores done, we'd go down to Pap Cockerham's pasture and play baseball. Me and my brother Sonny and Marcel Ledbetter and some of his brothers and sisters and a bunch more were down there playing baseball one afternoon, having such a fine time, and we messed up and let dark overtake us.

We were supposed to be home before dark. We were riding a little mustang horse named Toxie. As we got on Toxie, I got up behind my brother Sonny and we started going back to the house. Sonny started moaning, "Jerry, we got to go across that bridge that the headless man lives under."

We was some kind of scared.

Some of the older people in the community told us that there was a headless man that lived under the bridge. And at certain times, he'd come out from under there and get you. It always bothered me a little bit that he never would bother us according to the older people if we were going across that bridge to go to work or if we had to go across that bridge to plow. If we had to go across that bridge to go to school, he never would bother us.

But if we had to go across that bridge to play, that thing was bad and that headless man would come out from under there and get us.

Well, me and Sonny were dreading going over that bridge because it had gotten dark. That bridge was about a quarter of a mile from our house. We stopped about fifty yards from the bridge and my brother Sonny said, "Jerry, get ready. When we hit that bridge, this horse is gonna be running just as fast as she possibly can."

I had an old baseball cap on, and I turned that thing around where the bill would be sticking straight behind me and the wind wouldn't blow my cap off. I put my arms around my brother Sonny and laced my fingers right there in front of his belly, and I said, "Let's go. Have mercy, if you go fast enough, he won't be able to come out from under there and grab us. And if he gets in the road, maybe the horse will run over him."

Boogity, boogity, boogity, here we went. Just as we got to the edge of the bridge, Sonny took the line and hollered, "Hawww!"

Sonny slapped the horse and she made a lunge forward. My head was thrown back and the bill of that cap stuck me between my shoulder blades.

"Hawww!" I come just to screaming. "Hawww, Sonny, he's got me! Hewww, Lord, have mercy! Oh Lord, help me, Sonny, that thing's got me by the back of my neck."

Boogity, boogity, boogity we was going. Pulled up in the front yard and I jumped off that horse and ran in the house.

"Hawww, mama. Mama, mama, come quick, the headless man grabbed me by the back of my neck." And

I threw my head back and took my hand to show my mama where the headless man had grabbed me, and when I threw my head back, the bill of that cap stuck me again.

I paused, and I smiled a little bit. Mama said, "The headless man ain't got you. The bill of that cap stuck you back there."

Friends, had my mama not shown me that it was in fact the bill of that cap that struck me between my shoulder blades, I'd be writing in this book today, declaring before God, that he grabbed me. I knew he grabbed me and I'd go to my grave thinking there was something that came out from under that bridge and grabbed me back of my head.

I thought he had done it. But the fact that I thought it, didn't make it the truth.

8

Messin' Up

If you're fixing to make a decision about what's right and wrong in your life, do you ask other people's opinions about it?

That's a pretty good indication that you're fixing to mess up.

When I was a boy I was getting ready for a date one night. I walked into the side room and asked, "Mama, is my shirt dirty?"

"Son, if you're in doubt, it's dirty. Pull it off and get you another one."

So if you're fixing to do something and you want to know whether it's right or not: Number one, do you ask other people's opinions about it? Number two: do you argue with yourself?

I've spent many a mile on the highway arguing with Jerry that I ought to do a certain thing and I knew in my heart that I was lying. So if you argue with yourself, it's a pretty good indication that you should not do it.

Number three: do you feel uneasy when you do it? Had you just as soon that somebody not see you doing what it is that you've decided is all right for you to do?

Number four: can you give thanks and say, "Lord, I thank you for providing this for me"?

You've made up your mind you're going to do it, and the Bible says, "Give thanks for all things."

So while you do it, can you say, "Lord, thank you for providing this for me and I some kind of thank you for fixing it where I could commit what it is I'm doing"?

What is right or wrong? Do you ask other people? Do you argue with yourself? Do you feel uneasy when you do it? Can you give thanks to the Lord for providing it for you?

If you can't, you'd better watch out because you're fixing to mess up.

What a difference Jesus makes. Every day of my life I'm tempted. I've been able to overcome most temptations, because of the difference that Jesus Christ makes in my life.

Not too long ago my son was playing high school football. During one rainy night he attempted to kick an extra point, and it went off to the side.

"You knucklehead," yelled a man down in front of me as he jumped up. "Can't you even kick an extra point?"

And we had them 27 to 0 right then.

The minute he said "You knucklehead" and my young'un was the one he was hollering at, I felt my wife's hand come over on my leg and she said, "That's all right, honey. That's okay, Jerry; everything's fine, darling."

But I got up and I walked down there. "Sir, why did you call my young'un a knucklehead?"

You know what he said? "If he had kicked the extra point, I would have won my bet. I'm giving so many points."

"Fella, it's bad enough to bet on a horse or a dog. But when you bet on flesh and blood human beings, don't you bet on *my* young'un, and because you ain't gonna win some money in a bet, you call my boy a knucklehead. I want you to leave this stadium knowing one thing. I'm a Christian, and Jesus Christ has made a difference in my life to the extent that I ain't gonna whip you. But everywhere you go, you tell everybody you see that Jerry Clower would have whipped me but Jesus Christ made a difference in his life and he didn't. Sir, I ain't gonna lie to you. I am tempted to reach and get you in your Adam's apple and not only whip you but drag you around that track down there. But I'm not going to do it, and I praise God for the fact that I am a Christian and His grace is sufficient to keep me from making a fool out of myself."

The difference Jesus makes! Inasmuch as Jesus Christ makes this great difference, let's try to get Jesus preached to each and every lost individual on earth.

Last Easter I'm driving to church with my family and I tell my wife, "Darling, if there's a lost man sitting in the pew where I usually sit this morning, on Easter Sunday, I'll kneel down by him and pray or stand outside in the rain. He can have my seat. But if a Baptist is in my seat that ain't been there since last Easter, he's getting *up*."

"Honey, what in the world are the children going to think hearing you talk that way?"

"I'm saying it in front of the children because if they've got a like situation, I want them to get him out of their seat, too."

You know I say that facetiously, but I have to pray about things like that. I really do.

9

The Hunters

For some reason some of my favorite stories, and those my fans like best, are about hunters.

Like the time a big MCA record executive in Hollywood said, "Jerry, I sure would love to go bird hunting."

I told him the best quail hunting in the whole world is in southwest Mississippi. So he later flew to Jackson, and when he got off the jet, he had his hunting clothes on. He looked like Little Lord Fauntleroy.

We got in the car and went down to Route 4, Liberty, to the beautiful Virsi Ledbetter farm. I drove up into his yard. "Excuse me just a minute, sir, let me tell Uncle Virsi we're going to be hunting on his place."

I went in and Uncle Virsi was so glad to see me. "Welcome, son. I hope you kill a bunch of them."

"Thank you, Uncle Virsi."

I started out the door and Uncle Virsi started crying. "I'm gonna have to ask you to do something for me, son. Ol' Della, my mule, I made thirty good crops with her. The veterinarian was out here yesterday and said she's dying, and she's suffering. I just couldn't stand to see him put her to sleep yesterday. Jerry, would you shoot her for me?"

"Yeah, Uncle Virsi, I don't like to do it, but if she's suffering, I'll shoot her for you."

"You go ahead and shoot her and go on bird hunting, and me and the boys will tend to her late this evening."

On the way back to the car I thought, *I'm going to have me some fun out of this Hollywood dude.* I got in the car and said, "You know, that old scoundrel told me I couldn't hunt on his place? As good as I've been to him, he's told me, 'No—get you and that Hollywood city slicker away from here.'"

I beat the dashboard with my fists and I scratched off and threw rocks all up the side of his house, got on down the road about a hundred yards and there was old Della grazing. I slammed on the brakes. "Uh-huh, I'll show that old rascal."

I grabbed my shotgun and jumped out.

BOOM! BOOM!

And down old Della went, graveyard dead.

Just as I turned around and looked over to see what the dude thought, I heard three shots over there.

BOOM! BOOM! BOOM!

"What are you doing?" I yelled.

"That old fellow upset you so bad, Jerry, I killed three of his cows."

I attended the fiftieth wedding anniversary of Uncle Virsi Ledbetter and Aunt Pet, his wife. When I got there, Uncle Virsi's family had assembled. There they were: Ardel, Bernel, Raynel, W. L., Lanel, Odel, Marcel, New-Gene, Claude, and Clovis.

We had a great time. Everybody told Uncle Virsi and Aunt Pet how much we loved them.

Then New-Gene Ledbetter became the spokesman. He got up and said, "Poppa, we want you to know that for years and years you have been trying to catch the old Bad Daddy Coon down in the swamps—Old Slantface. Tonight, in a wheelchair, we're going to take you coonhunting."

Now, word was out that Uncle Virsi wasn't quite as crippled as he made out like he was. But he enjoyed his grandchildren pushing him around in that wheelchair.

Come dark, everybody got the carbide lights on, put 'em on their heads, lit them, got on their overalls and their coonhunting clothes. We put Uncle Virsi back up in the back of the pickup truck and went down a log road.

"Poppa, we've done found the Bo Coon's den. We know where it is. We're going to drive you down into the woods and stop you. If they tree any raccoon, we're going to try to weave you down in there. And your wedding anniversary present will be that you can say that you went coonhunting. We're taking you to the woods."

We got down there and old Highball, Jr. struck a trail right off. AAAOOO! And Old Brumey's puppies, and old Red and little Spot and Queen. AAAOOO! "Look for 'em."

It was beautiful. They treed just like that. New-Gene drove the pickup down this log road until the bumper of it touched the trunk of the tree where they had treed the raccoon.

The big tree was slanted over an old slough. A little creek used to run under there.

"All right, boys, he's up in there. See if you can shine his eyes."

We went to shining those lights. Directly New-Gene said, "I see him; I see him."

The eyes looked as wide apart as the length of a hammer handle.

"Somebody climb the tree!" Uncle Virsi yelled. He was just jumping up and down on the wheelchair. "Climb the tree. Punch him out! Punch him out!"

Clovis said, "Poppa, don't you remember how New–Gene can mock a female raccoon? And if that's the old bad one, he might walk down the tree."

"Go ahead, New–Gene, let's see."

New–Gene made his female raccoon noise.

"Waaaooo, that thing's moving, y'all watch it. That thing's big as a dog. It *is* old Slantface. It *is* the Bad Daddy Coon, what we've been trying to catch all our life!"

That thing walked down that tree and jumped up on the hood of that pickup, up over the windshield with all those dogs right in behind him. He'd just slap one of them. He was a bad thing.

Everybody was hollering, whooping, and screaming. That thing got over there in the back of that pickup and the wheelchair turned bottom up.

"Get poppa, get poppa!"

New–Gene was still making those raccoon noises.

"Shut up, New–Gene! You done made that thing mad enough! Don't do that no more."

All of the lights went out, the dogs were howling and with that raccoon hollering, you ain't never heard such a ruckus in all your life. The lights of the pickup went out. And it got deathly quiet.

Can't find Uncle Virsi.

The wheelchair has turned bottom upwards in the creek. Clovis is beginning to squall and holler, "Where's my poppa?"

We waded out into the slough and felt for Uncle Virsi. He ain't there; the dogs ain't there.

When we got back to the house, we appointed Clovis

to tell Aunt Pet that on this momentous occasion Uncle Virsi couldn't be found. That he was missing.

Clovis ran in the house squalling, "Mama, I hate to tell you, but we can't find poppa."

"You can't find poppa?" she said. "I reckon not. He's in the bedroom asleep. He got home before the dogs."

10

What's Wrong with Our Country?

Everywhere I go, I'm asked this question.

I'll be thrown in with a few folks and they'll show me around and go to talking about what's wrong with the country and what's wrong with their town. After being with some people for an hour or so, they look at me and say in a gruff voice, "What's wrong with our country?"

A lot of times I'm tempted to grab them in the throat and say, "You." Because they go to telling me what they're doing to make the country right.

What's wrong with the country, whatever it is, can be righted only by each individual righting himself or herself. Sometimes we try to straighten out things by getting the masses to react to it at one time. But if you can get individuals to straighten themselves out, then they make up the masses and you've got it done.

Here are a few recommendations.

There ain't so much wrong with the country as some

folks think there is. But we can have a better country if each individual citizen simply dedicated himself or herself to being a better citizen. Folks ought to be good citizens.

A lot of times you hear some learned folks telling us to be good citizens, but they don't tell us what it is you need to do to be a good citizen.

Here are some earmarks of a good citizen: Suppose Jerry Clower moved to where you live and took up residence in your city. Let me tell you some things I would do in order to be a good citizen.

First, I'd hunt up and seek out the church of my faith, put my membership in that church, and make them a good hand. Yes, this is the first thing I'd do.

Now if I moved to this town on a Saturday night, the next Lord's day, which would be the next morning, I'd be found in the church of my faith putting my membership in that church. I'd start off each week by attending God's house, and I would start off being a good citizen. That would be the first thing.

The reason I would hunt up and seek out my particular church, Southern Baptist Church, is because I'm a Christian. An individual can do better in a church than he can do out.

The next thing I'd do is, I would become a qualified elector. In other words, I'd register and vote and take part in elections.

If my next door neighbor didn't know how to instruct me on how to become qualified to vote, I'd ask some person running for public office and he'd get me by the arm and lead me down to wherever the place is that you register and show me how to do it, and I'd do it. I'd register, take part in elections, and vote.

I've gone all over this country making the statement, even on national television, that I think young people today are better than they were when I was growing up, and I still believe that.

But there is one thing that the young people have really disappointed me in and that was after they took to the streets and lobbied and did a lot of things to show their disgust that young people eighteen years of age cannot vote. Well, the power-that-be corrected this and fixed it so eighteen-year-olds could vote. But then, didn't but half of the eighteen-year-olds register, and then didn't but half of those that registered go to the polls and vote. And this is tragic.

In some instances, blacks have been shot down in cold blood, right in front of their little children. Blood ran all over the carport where they were murdered. One of the main things they were advocating was the right to vote.

My, what a price some blacks paid in order to get it corrected to where they could go register, vote, and even run for public office.

Now, today, I've heard some outstanding black leaders recommend publicly, "Well, just let the blacks stay away from the polls, because there's nobody running that we think is the man that we ought to support."

Aw, how tragic this is! To be a good citizen, you ought to get involved and certainly take part in elections and vote.

And I go one step further.

If you are not a qualified elector, if you aren't registered and you can't vote and you don't vote, I would suggest you shut up griping about what's going on in this country. You don't have the right to open your mouth about anything.

I'm not saying different folks would be elected if everybody registered and voted. I don't believe that at all.

I'm not one of these people who run around all over

73

the country saying all politicians are crooked. There are more statesmen and people trying to do a good job in politics than there are that's not trying to do a good job. I'm firmly convinced of that.

One of the main problems in politics is littleness and backbiting—politicians in the legislature arguing with one another. But, basically, most of them are not in it for personal gain. They're in it to try to make a good public servant, and that's what they got into it for—and I'm not one to say they are all crooked.

To be a good citizen, the next thing that I would do is to serve on the jury if I was asked to serve.

A lot of scalawags and scoundrels are running free. One of the reasons they're running free, in my opinion, is because good people were too busy to serve on the jury. They just make up lies and tell the judge, "I can't serve."

I've often said that Mississippi Chemical Corporation, the company I spent most of my life working for, is a company with a heart. They even have a policy where, if an employee is called to jury duty, his pay goes on just like he was working.

Man alive! If we could get other corporations, companies, and employers throughout the United States to put this fine country-loving policy in their overall company policies, what a great move for good citizenship and justice this would be. Yes, if you're asked to serve on the jury, you ought to serve and you ought to make a decision on evidence presented, not on who's rich or who's poor and so forth.

The next thing I'd do to be a good citizen would be to invest some money in some local industry, whatever the size of my town. Especially if it was a small town and needed a good industry. I'd try to band myself together with other business people and invest some money in a local industry.

74

What's Wrong with Our Country?

You know, it's a funny thing. Some people will fight that New York Stock Exchange, and that's perfectly all right with me. And they do a lot of investing and keep it a secret from their wife and their bankers. Especially when they lose a bunch of money. But they'll invest in a local industry—one that was started in their own home state by good folks—and if it doesn't pay 20 percent the first six months, they'll walk from one end of the state to the other cussing everybody in it. This is not being consistent.

Yes, in order to be a good citizen, an individual ought to start off the first day of every week in the church of his faith worshiping God. Next, make sure you are a qualified elector and you do vote. Next, serve on the jury if you're asked to serve. And last, but not least, invest some money in a local industry.

Being a good citizen is the right of all people. Earlier in this chapter I mentioned how some people really sacrificed to get the right to do something, but then didn't do it. I can't quite understand some people's actions, including some of my black friends.

We went through some troubled times with school integration, and we got it done. Then it wasn't long before I read in the paper where some group at a university was demanding that the school let them have an all-black dormitory. My soul, we apparently just can't understand what freedom is!

One of the best illustrations of bigotry and racism in this country today is the black caucus in the United States Congress. Why in the world do they have to meet as a group of blacks and call themselves the black caucus, when for years and years folks have suffered, bled, and died to do away with the white caucus?

There's no Italian caucus in Congress. They don't have a Polish caucus, so I don't think they ought to have a black caucus.

LET THE HAMMER DOWN!

There ought to be representatives who make up the Senate and the House who are members of the Congress and as individuals band themselves together to govern right. Any law that's passed is passed for all Americans and you don't need any little group to oversee anything. The black caucus is an act of bigotry and racism. I have been trying to help stamp out these evils for many years of my life.

As I travel over this great country, I've discovered a real problem is able-bodied folks who are able to work but they're too lazy to work. Now I don't want anybody getting on television and saying it's the establishment and it's my fault that a fellow is lazy, because that would be a bald-faced lie.

I am not lazy, and I am part of the establishment. And because a fellow won't work and is lazy, is his fault. It ain't my fault, and I don't want it pinned on me.

It's real simple. I agree with the Apostle Paul in the word of God. He said that folks who are able to work and won't work ought not to eat. I'd like to see that law passed just as soon as Congress can get it enacted and get the President to sign it. Now I'm not knocking folks who aren't able to work. I'm not knocking the folks who diligently want work and can't find it. Very few papers I pick up haven't got ads in there wanting people to work.

A contractor friend of mine told me that he needed some laborers and went by the employment service and told them he could use a bunch of workers. In a week's time, fifty-two laborers came by the job, and all of them left but two. And the biggest majority of them when they got there . . . they would be told, "Let's build this scaffold. Pick up that board right there."

And they'd say, "You mean I got to pick up a board? I ain't gonna do that." And then they'd leave the job and they'd go back to get their unemployment.

Look, this is a bad precedent. This reminds me of a true story. And, oh, how true this story is!

There was a lady who lived in the state of Mississippi who had a pet squirrel. That squirrel was beautiful. Neighbors would go watch the little squirrel sit in its cage and, with its teeth, burst the hulls from around the nuts, especially pecans. Then the squirrel would eat the meat of the nut.

One day the lady who owned the squirrel was shopping in the supermarket and saw a bag of shelled pecans. There they were in a beautiful bag, a little cellophane bag, and you could see the beautiful halves of the pecans. She said, "My, look at that, my little old squirrel won't have to burst them old hulls no more to get something to eat. I'll buy my little squirrel the pecans."

Everything was fine. But in a few weeks, the little squirrel was sick. The lady carried the squirrel to the veterinarian, and the vet said, "My goodness, this squirrel's front teeth are growing too long. What's wrong, what are you feeding this squirrel?"

"Shelled pecans."

"You mean to tell me you're feeding this squirrel pecans that have already been hulled? Lady, don't you know that God made this creature to work for its food? That's part of nature for this squirrel to open up nuts with its teeth. You've got to stop putting pecans in that cage that have been shelled."

The lady did, but the little squirrel turned its nose up at the pecans. He'd found another way. Haaw, somebody taking care of him. He wasn't going to bust them old pecans and work for his food any more. Little squirrel wouldn't bust those pecans. Little squirrel wouldn't eat. So the lady started giving it the pecans that were already shelled so it wouldn't die, but the squirrel's teeth had grown so long that the squirrel couldn't chew and the little squirrel laid down and died graveyard dead. Yes,

77

the lady loved the little squirrel. She loved it so much she killed it.

Able-bodied folks who are able to work, ought to go to work. That would help this country a great, great deal. The Bible says to make your living by the sweat of your brow. It's honorable to work, and people respect an individual who's not lazy. Get out there on the job and, whatever it is, do it to the best of your ability and let the hammer down.

L. to R.: Barbara Farnsworth, my Nashville agent; me; Charles McKeller, Top Billing's man in Mississippi; Judy Denson, Jackson (Miss.) TV personality; and my manager, Tandy Rice, president of Top Billing of Nashville.

Here I am doing what I shouldn't do.

Dr. Paul Stevens, bossman of Southern Baptist Radio and Television Commission, and Lady Byrd Johnson with me at last year's Abe Lincoln Awards Banquet. We were winners.

One of my closest friends and my pilot, Jim Rupe, producer of award-winning "Country Crossroads" radio show. *Rachel Colvin photo.*

My manager and me . . . real happy . . . receiving a Platinum album in 1977 from MCA Records. This signifies sales in excess of 1,000,000 units and was a first for the label in the "talking records" category. *Bob Schanz photo.*

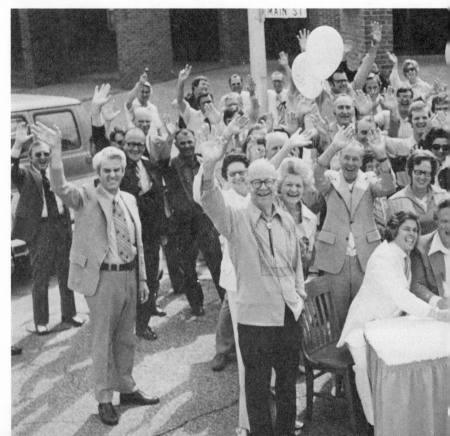

President Carter stayed with the Owen Coopers when he was in Yazoo City. Here's a picture of me and the Coopers.

ain Street, Yazoo City, Mississippi, on signing of my new MCA contract

Jerry Reed loved my daughter Katy the minute he saw her, and she loved him too. *Marion Currie photo.*

I love Foy Valentine like a brother.

Me with Debbie Reynolds on the David Frost Show.

I do lots of banquets and conventions every year. Here
I am at a typical performance.

II

The Chauffeur Knows Best

A big oil firm had their annual meeting in a big hotel down in Houston, Tex. They got this Ph.D. fellow from way up in the Midwest to come down and make a speech.

Folks, he forevermore made a speech. It so inflamed and enthused those oil folks that they called their executive committee together and said, "Let's hire that fellow and put him out on the road making this same speech. Wherever he can gather up a crowd, let him talk to them."

They did. They bought him a big car and got him a chauffeur with a blue serge suit. And this man started traveling all over the country making this speech.

After they'd been doing this about eight months, they were driving down the road one day and the chauffeur looked in the rear view mirror and said, "Professor."

"What?" asked the professor.

"There ain't no fairness in this country."

"My good man, why would you make a statement like that?"

"I can make that cottonpicking speech as good as you can. I'm barely making a living on what y'all are paying me, and you're getting rich."

"Sir, I want you to know that I've got my B.S. degree—"

"Don't start on about all them things. I ain't interested in them. I've heard you make that speech once a day for eight months. I've done memorized it. I'm a better speechmaker than you are and I can make the cottonpicking speech better than you can."

"Well, I'm fixing to go to a major university and they've never seen me. They don't even know what I look like. You pull over to the roadside park up here. We're about the same size and we'll trade clothes. We'll put you up there on the stage and let you make the speech, and I'll be the chauffeur and sit out in the audience, and I'll watch you make a fool out of yourself. That suits me fine. Let's change clothes."

So they drive up to the big university, the real professor with the blue serge suit on driving the car, and the chauffeur sitting on the back seat with a little briefcase in his lap. Standing room only—22,000 people—in the fieldhouse. The great Ph.D. that graduated from the great school of minds was coming to speak.

They introduced him. And as he got up there to speak, there was the real professor sitting on the back row with the hardbilled chauffeur's cap in his lap, peeping at him.

Talk about making a speech! He forevermore shelled down the corn. He shucked it right on down to the cob. They throwed their books in the air, wallowed on the floor, hollered, gave him a standing ovation, screamed. They finally got order restored.

The president of the school got up and said, "Well, we have about ten minutes before the bell rings. I wonder if y'all would like to ask this gentleman any questions."

You've seen the type: a fellow got up about halfway back. Big horn-rimmed glasses on—a real egghead. Had books under each arm. "Professor, if one of those dinosaurs that roamed the earth two billion years ago died and his carcass rotted and the earth's atmosphere built up layer after layer after layer to 5,986 feet, and two billion years later a drill bit drilling a well on a wildcat venture bores through this decayed carcass, what will the PH of the soil be that's contained in the core of the drillbit and what will be the name of the stratosphere?"

This fellow just stood there and looked at him. You could have heard a pin drop.

"Student, as long as I've been in this business that's about the most simplest question I've ever been asked since I've been speaking. I'm surprised that they'd let a man who don't know no more than you know get in this university. Just to show you how simple the question is, my chauffeur is in the back of the room and I'll ask him to stand up and answer it."

12

Fight Satan, Not People

The greatest way to fight Satan is to kill him with love.

Love.

Don't think Satan ain't real. He is real. He goes around trying to mess up folks. Don't ever tell me he doesn't, because I've done business with him.

He is so cunning and so skilled and so smart. He knows how to trip folks, knows how to mess them up. He starts off with some insignificant, little bitty thing, and he gets you to participate in it a little bit at a time; then before you know it, you're doing it regularly. And what you're doing is bad and you're messing up and Satan's tickled. He's got you.

One of the best ways to fight Satan is to be actively involved in a New Testament church. I marvel at the strength, when I go sit down in the church house among worshipers, sing the hymns, fellowship with God's people, and hear a sermon. It just gives me strength to fight Satan.

The church can compete with the world. You better believe it. Those who are Spirit-filled can compete with the world.

I'm so proud. I thank God every day for my own home church. Not long ago I called in my Sue when she was fourteen years old and said, "Darling, daddy don't get to spend as much time with you as he would like to. I'm off on the road in show business. But I'm fixing to go to Hollywood to do the Academy of Country Music Awards.

"I'm gonna fly out there in a big jet airplane. And when I get there, MCA Records is gonna meet daddy in a limousine, the same kind that Elton John rides around in. And I've talked to Ms. Joan Bullard, who is head of publicity for MCA, and she's promised me if you want to visit with Elton John and some other artists on the MCA label, she'll arrange that while we're in Hollywood.

"And, Sue, you get your closest friend, and daddy's gonna pay her way out there, too, and we'll stay at the Universal Sheraton. You'll get to sit at the table with Mel Tillis, and you'll get to meet Mr. Lorne Greene, David Janssen, and Dinah Shore. You'll see a great host of other stars and it'll just be something. You're gonna go on a VIP tour of Universal Studios in Hollywood and, Sue, daddy's so glad that I can arrange this trip for you and your friend. It's gonna make me feel real good that I can take you out there."

Friends, my Sue paused, looked at me and said, "Daddy, I love you and I'm so glad that you would arrange it to where me and one of my friends could go on this trip, but daddy, there's something going on at the church activities building I don't want to miss. I won't be able to go with you this time."

Wheew! Tears welled up in my eyes. My heart beat heavy in my breast with joy. And I said, "Praise God from whom all blessings flow."

Yes, the church of the living God can compete with the world and make the gospel and fellowshiping with God's people just as interesting as any other form of entertainment. Get it on, dear ones. If you're in your church and you're dragging your feet, you're letting Satan get in amongst it. He's tickled because you haven't had enough faith to ask God to let you get something started that would make worshiping the living God more interesting than some other things that you could be doing. If that's the case then I'm praying for you.

But the devil, wheew, he is mighty. A good illustration of how the devil deals with us and tricks folks, is what happened when I was a little boy growing up at Route 4, Liberty, Mississippi. In the fall of the year when the folks got all of their cotton picked and all the corn pulled and sweet potatoes dug and their sugar cane banked, everybody used to just turn the hogs out and let them run in the woods and eat acorns.

That used to bother me and my brother Sonny. That grieved us very, very much. Every time Big Daddy would raise the bottom rail on that hog pen and let the hogs out, we would near about cry.

Me and Sonny would say, "We ain't never gonna get to see them hogs again."

But Big Daddy would explain to us. "Babies, you see, your granddaddy has got a notch. In my hog's ears I put one notch and the notch stands for 'this hog belongs to Wesley Burns.' Now there are other hogs in the woods, and if you find a hog that's got two notches in his ears, that simply says 'this hog belongs to Mr. Ben Newman.' And if you find a hog that's got three notches in his ear, that simply means that 'this hog belongs to Mr. Archie Pray.' "

When folks started their early spring plowing and would be getting ready to plant a crop, you had to get those hogs up. And my grandpa, Big Daddy, Mr. Wesley Burns, used to stick ears of corn in his overall pockets, and me and my brother Sonny would go with him. He'd go down to the edge of the swamp, and he'd tear the shucks on one of the ears of corn and he'd say, "Piiig, pig, pig, pig, pig pigooo." Then there'd be this chewing sound.

"Pig, pig, pig. . . ."

"Chomp, chomp, chomp."

"Pig, pig, pig, pig."

And there would come those hogs. Now if Big Daddy threw down a whole ear of corn, that hog would grab that ear of corn and run way back in the swamp and lay down on its belly and eat the corn and the hog would have gotten away from us.

But Big Daddy didn't do that. He put down two or three grains at a time, and when the hog would eat those two or three grains of corn he'd look up and Big Daddy would say, "Chomp, chomp, chomp," and put down three more grains, and then he'd start walking back toward the house. He'd say, "Pig, pig, pig," and he'd put down a few more grains of corn. The hog would eat that corn and follow him all the way to the house. When he got to the house, he had already fixed a slip-gap. Put a stick of firewood up under the second rail of the hog pen where the hogs could go through that opening into the hog pen. And when Big Daddy would get to the house he would throw all that corn that he had left in his overall jumper pocket over in that pen and the hogs would rush through that opening, grab an ear of corn, and turn to come out. But Big Daddy would kick that chock out and "Wham"—he had 'em. He had them hogs.

Then we'd get over in there, and all the hogs that

had the wrong notches in the ear and didn't belong to Big Daddy, we'd fix it so we could get them out of that pen.

But he tempted the hogs, one step at a time, all the way to that pen. And do you know where those hogs would end up? In a barrel of scalding hot water with their throats cut.

Satan, he's got hog pens built all over this country. And he isn't tempting folks just with tremendous temptations all at the same time because he won't get them. They'll overcome that. Awww, but he'll serve something up for you just to look at or to get a little nibble of, and you'll take one step at a time. And, ultimately, it may lead up to a broken home or your children thrown away. It'll end up about the same penalty as being thrown in a big vat of scalding hot water with your throat cut. That's the way the devil does it. The devil tempts us one step at a time, and that's the way he gets us.

There's a story about some Indians up in Canada. They wanted to figure out a way to get some of those big Canadian honkers. Catch them, roast them, and eat them.

But they didn't have guns, and the geese were swimming out in the middle of the river. All the Indians had to do was just walk to the edge and the wild honkers would fly off.

The Indians got to thinking how in the world they could catch some of these big old Canadian honkers. That sure would be a good meal.

Well, they went way up stream and got some small gourds, little bitty gourds that they were growing. A round gourd. Looks just like the gourds that Mexican musicians shake on television when they make that music. They'd put a few of them in that river, and as the geese would be swimming in the middle of the river, the little gourds would just come floating right by them and the geese didn't pay any attention to them.

In a few days they'd get a little bigger gourd, and in a few more days they'd get one just a little bigger. The geese didn't notice since it was a gradual increase in the size of the gourds. They never paid attention to them.

One day, the gourd got big enough for the Indian to cut out the bottom side of it, slip it over his head, tread water and come easing down that river with the gourd over the upper part of his body. As that gourd eased by one of those geese, the Indian would just catch him by the feet and snatch him down under the water. As much as he squalled or flopped his wings, he was deep enough that he never even disturbed the other geese.

As the Indian got on down, he'd grab another one and pull him down under the water. Then he'd stay in that gourd and ease way on down the river.

Any time the Indians wanted to capture a goose, all they had to do was to get in one of the gourds and ease down the river and pluck 'em just like the devil plucks— gradually, one step at a time. Just like sin increasing a little bit more each day as we go along and then, WHAM!, the devil's got us.

The geese ended up in a pot of scalding water. That's what happened to them.

Another way to fight old Satan is to keep your testimony fresh. Practice it.

The best way to witness and tell others about Christ is to tell them what has happened to you. Have you ever been saved? Are you on the road to heaven? Well, if you are, tell it!

There have been a lot of books written on soul winning, and I praise God for every word that's ever been written about how to spread the gospel. The best way to do it is to keep it simple. Just tell other folks what has happened to you.

Now let me clear up something. You can't tell other people what's happened to you if it ain't never happened, no more than you can tell them how to get back from a place you've never been.

But it's real simple. Tell it. Get it on. Tell people! As you tell them, this will strengthen your faith. It will keep your testimony fresh.

About twenty years ago, I was selling fertilizer in a little country store in Pike County, Mississippi. This young Baptist preacher, who had been to seminary, was starting out a career and was preaching at a rural church out in the country. I didn't know him. Never heard of him before.

He stopped at the country store to pick up something. While I was in there talking to the fellow and was going to sell him a few bags of the product I was selling, there was another man in the store, and we started talking about the Lord. I read him some scriptures and told him how I became a Christian at the East Fork Baptist Church at age 13.

The man said he'd like to be a believer, and accepted Christ.

Last year, over twenty years later, I was being introduced by one of the great Baptist preachers of our nation, Dr. C. C. Randall, pastor of the First Baptist Church of Tuscaloosa, Alabama. When he introduced me, he told in detail of how he was a young Baptist preacher and stopped at a country store years ago and saw a young salesman winning a man to Jesus in the back of the store. And that salesman was Jerry Clower. He told how he had watched me grow from that on into show business.

Folks, I thought my heart was going to burst with joy.

Now, do you think that strengthened my faith? Do you think my boldness and witnessing to that fellow helped this preacher C. C. Randall years ago when he saw a Baptist layman who loved the Lord enough and who had faith enough to witness for Christ? Do you think that strengthened him? You better believe it strengthened him.

When folks see your boldness, then they'll get bold for the Lord. Yes, one of the best ways to fight Satan is to be faithful to God.

I marvel at the faithfulness of God. Wheew! My own pastor, Rev. Jim Yates, was a young married man traveling from Brownsville, Tennessee, in his early preaching days. He was riding the train all night to get to the seminary up at Louisville, Kentucky, to get his education. In Louisville, he stayed with his wife's grandmother, who didn't live too far from the Baptist Theological Seminary.

He did this back and forth, riding that train. The young preacher boy, there on weekends preaching the Word, visiting the flock, and then catching that train going back up there to get the education, living with his wife's grandmother.

Well, friends, just as he got his degree from the seminary, the grandmother died and the L&N Railroad stopped running that train. Think of that. I marvel at the faithfulness of God.

Just the other day we had some rare weather here in Yazoo City. I was supposed to do a show on a Thursday night in Houma, Louisiana, and the next night in Seminole, Oklahoma. My schedule called for me to get up early and drive my Dodge pickup truck to Jackson, Mississippi Airport, fly to New Orleans and on to Houma, then back up to New Orleans and then to Seminole.

Wednesday night I called the Mississippi Highway Patrol and Officer Bell answered the phone and said, "Jerry, you can't drive on those icy highways to Jackson in the morning. There's no way you can."

"Officer, I've got to get to Houma. They've sold the tickets. It's a sellout. I can't stand them up."

"Jerry, we don't want anything to happen to you. Make some other kind of arrangements."

I hung up the phone. Sitting at the supper table, I prayed, "Lord, whatever I need to do, show me. I'm on your side."

And then my mind went to Jim Rupe, a man who belongs to a flying club in Fort Worth, Texas. He's my dear friend, and a qualified instrument rated pilot. I thought, I'll just call Jim and get him to lease an airplane and come over here in the morning, get me and fly me to Houma; then I'll fly back to Dallas with him and fly out of there the next morning to go on to Seminole, Oklahoma.

When I dialed Jim's number, the line was busy. I dialed it again in about five minutes and the line was busy.

I popped off to my wife, saying, "I'm gonna get Jim Rupe's two little girls a telephone put in their room and just have the bill sent to me every month, so when I want to call Jim under some of these icy road emergencies, I can get him on the phone."

I dialed him again and the line was still busy. I spent thirty minutes dialing him.

Well, I marvel at the faithfulness of God. Thank God, his line was busy. Because I got to thinking, well let me call Larry Wells, one of the Mississippi Chemical pilots, and see if even Jim Rupe's plane can land here in the morning and pick me up.

When I called Larry, he said, "Yes, he can land even on the ice because he can reverse the props and use them to stop the plane. But, Jerry, the Mississippi Chemical plane is going to Pascagoula tomorrow. We're going empty because we're going down there to pick up some folks."

"Wheew! I'll get you all to drop me off at Houma."

Why, we had a 100-mile-an-hour tail wind the next morning. We went to New Orleans in a little over 30 minutes, and I was right on schedule.

Think of that! Had Jim Rupe's phone not been busy, I'd have leased a big airplane that would have cost a lot of money. But since his phone was busy, everything worked out beautifully. I marvel at the faithfulness of God. God listens.

Most of us pray, "Lord, if it be thy will, do it." Well, that's a cop out. See, if it isn't done, then what we'll do is say, "Well, Lord, it wasn't your will." If we want something and we actually believe it, we say, "Lord, thy will be done. And we know your will is that you grant things and we're fixing to get it on and pray right and get it done."

A dear friend, J. T. Grantham, has been an old Gideon buddy for over twenty years. He's in the investment business. He told me the story of how he was going up the highway and there was a hitchhiker.

There's so much meanness going on in the world that you don't know whether to stop and pick up a hitchhiker or not. J. T. Grantham passed this fellow on the road and got two miles up the road before he got under the conviction that he ought to go back and pick him up. So he turned around and went back and picked him up and was giving him a ride on up north on I-55 toward Canton, Mississippi.

J. T. started talking to him, and the discussion got around to J. T. telling him about Jesus. He witnessed to him. Tears came to this man's eyes and he looked at J. T. Grantham and said, "My mama before she died used to pray that somebody would talk to me and tell me the salvation story just like you're telling me now."

J. T. looked at that fellow and said, "I marvel at the faithfulness of God."

Here's a godly mama gone home to glory, and yet God's answering her prayer. And it impressed that fellow. J. T. Grantham won this man to Jesus.

The faithfulness of God, how wonderful it is!

Through all of this, Satan would have us to complicate it so folks can't understand it.

Another way to fight Satan is to keep it simple. Keep it simple. Don't let Satan lead you to be something you ain't and mess up and complicate something that's simple.

One of the real people I've loved for a long time is Dr. Bill Davis. He is something!

He was the man who was instrumental, whose leadership was instrumental, in helping black preachers get an education in the state of Mississippi. He's a Baptist preacher, and I remember hearing him preach.

I don't know why, but I feel like some of my black friends can express themselves better than some of my white friends, because they keep it simple.

Dr. Davis tells a true story about this. It happened more than fifty years ago. He had been an ordained minister about a month. His white friends would say, "Oh, Brother Davis, I'm so thrilled that God has called you into his marvelous work." Or people would say, "Oh, I'm so thrilled that you have surrendered to preach the gospel."

All of this is fine, but look and listen to this: After he'd been an ordained minister for about a month, a black lady walked up to him and said, "I hear you are a light–toter."

"What did you say?"

"I hear you have been called to tote the light."

"That's right," Dr. Davis said.

She looked him right in the eyes, put her hands on his shoulders, and commanded, "Hear me, hear me. Hear until you know what I am saying. 'Lessen you tote the light and tote it right, you won't tote it at all.' Now get at it! Get the job done. Now tote the light and tote it right for the glory of God."

Dr. Davis says that through fifty-five years of preaching the words of that dear black lady have challenged him. When he gets a little despondent, and when the devil gets after him, it seems he can hear that godly black woman saying, "Now get at it! Get the job done. Tote the light and tote it right for the glory of God."

Now improve on this if you will. How can you better describe what God wants a preacher to do than *tote the light?* Keep it simple. Satan would have you to complicate stuff, and folks won't be able to understand what you're saying.

At the beginning of this book, I explained how I defined *Let the Hammer Down.* I quoted from the late, great George Washington Carver who said, "Do the best you can with what you got, and do it now."

As far as Dr. Carver is concerned, I marvel at the faithfulness of God.

Do you realize that in the last year of the Civil War, some slave–nappers took from the Moses Carver farm near Diamond Grove, Missouri, a black woman and her infant son? Carver sent hunters who chased the kidnapers to Arkansas. They found the baby, but not the mother. They took the baby back to the Moses Carver farm in a saddle bag.

For nine years, that black boy named George Washington Carver lived in Moses Carver's home. He was a little bitty boy, and he did household chores. He learned to sew, knit, cook, quilt, garden, and to do other things which cultivated his quick mind and agile hands.

When he was nine, he was sent out to work as a houseboy. There he attended a country school and was befriended by a black woman named Mother Maria Watkins, who gave him his first copy of the Bible. He read the Bible with great interest. In fact, he began to memorize passages about the earth and growing things. Later he salted and peppered his addresses on botany and agriculture with biblical passages committed to memory.

One time Carver needed some paint for a barn over there in Tuskegee, and they didn't have any. He said, "That soil's red, and I believe I can figure out a way to get that red coloring out of the soil and make some paint."

And he did. And they painted the barn and painted some fences.

Beautiful.

But, ladies and gentlemen, George Washington Carver, my soul, was called the Wizard of Tuskegee. He found uses for peanuts in more than 300 products. He found over 125 uses for sweet potatoes.

Dr. George Washington Carver. He let the hammer down!

13

Ain't God Good!

What? A chapter with the same title as my first book?

Yeah. What's wrong with that? Especially when the chapter deals with all the wonderful letters that my first book inspired.

Like I said before, a lot more people love me a $1.75 worth than $6.95 worth, and I can't say I really blame them. When Word Books published my first book, the reaction from the readers was immediate. Then when the paperback version came out from good ole Simon & Schuster, it was like an avalanche. Letters came from everywhere. And that's great.

One of the features of the first book that drew a lot of compliments was the chapter about all of the letters I receive. This gives you a chance to see not only what I'm about, but what my fans are about.

It was so popular that I'm going back to the well and doing it again. My co-writer, Gerry Wood, has selected what he thought were some of the strongest letters I've received.

LET THE HAMMER DOWN!

I get hundreds of letters a week, and so many of them have poured in recently from people who have read *Ain't God Good!* in the hardback or paperback edition.

Man, is it a good feeling to know that people can read what I write and better their lives because of it! I've witnessed the power of God from the pulpit, from the stage of the Grand Ole Opry, and from my MCA and Word records. But this is the first time I've been able to enjoy this power from a book. Oh, how happy it makes me to know that these peoples' lives have been touched—and sometimes changed—by a simple book from me!

These are more than letters. Some are actually short stories and human dramas. So I've included several of them because they make for fascinating reading:

Dear Mr. Clower:

I have just finished your book, *Ain't God Good!* Over the years I have read a lot of books, but nothing quite like this.

In the beginning of the book I perhaps was skeptical about a man really telling it like it is. By the time I had read the last chapter, I knew I had read the life story of a man who not only told it like it was, but a man who loves God and his fellowman.

One would not have to worry about their children reading this book. You can put it right out in front. I must say in reading it I laughed, I cried, and above all I really enjoyed the book as a whole.

In closing may I say that the best part of the book to me was your description of Christmas. Thank you for writing the book. May God bless and keep.

Yours in Christian fellowship,
Rev. William Matthews, Moultrie, Georgia

Dear Jerry,

I have just finished reading your book, *Ain't God Good!*, and would like to thank you for a masterpiece in human emotion. . . . Your book is a refreshing breath of spring air in today's bookstores. I really enjoyed sharing with you some of the times of your life.

Most of all I would like to thank you for giving me the courage through God to pursue my life's ambition. I've always wanted to be a dentist, and after four years in the Navy I started in school. I was thinking of dropping out because of money problems, but I got your book for a Christmas present from my wife, and after reading it and thinking over some of the things you said, I know that if I put my faith in the Lord, everything will turn out all right. For this I thank you.

Thanks again for your encouragement.

Tom Slusser, Independence, Kansas

Dear Jerry,

Thank you for one of the nicest, most heart-warming experiences I can recall. I have just finished reading your happy book, *Ain't God Good!*

With all the heartache, disillusionments, and problems so frequently attributed to folks in the entertainment field, you, your country humor, and your witnessing for Christ are like a breath of fresh air after a spring shower. *Most* refreshing!

No better emissary could our Lord have chosen to show the joy, the fun, the pride, and the sincere honesty of His way of life.

Dare we to hope there may be more of your wonderful books forthcoming? I sincerely hope so!

May you and your beloved Homerline continue receiving God's blessings and may you rest secure in the palm of His hand. Thank you again for the opportunity of reading your joyful philosophy.

> Sincerely,
> Mrs. Grace M. Hormel, Kerman, California

Dear Jerry,

I made a big mistake yesterday.

I bought a copy of that book what you done wrote. Yesterday was one of my very busiest days. At noon I picked up your book intending to read only the Preface. That was the second mistake. I never got one other thing done the rest of the day. I can't believe I read the whole thing.

I laughed a little and cried a little. My staff thought I had gone nuts. There were times when I said "Amen" and times when my hackles bristled a bit. Thanks for saying some things that needed to be said.

I've got to get to work and see if I can get caught up on what I didn't do yesterday.

> Keep The Son Shining,
> Gene Dobbs
> Pastor, McLaurin Baptist Church
> Pearl, Mississippi

Dear Jerry,

You are the talk of Seminole, Oklahoma!!! Your performance at the Chamber of Commerce banquet was the best thing we have done for this town in a long time.

After you left Friday morning I came back to the office and began to read your book (it was out in paperback here in Seminole Friday). Never have I read anything that moved me quite as much as that book. It has been a blessing to my life and meeting you really added special meaning to the book.

My daughter Deborah could not believe that she got to actually meet you, and the ice cream cone that you bought her in Shawnee made her a hero at school the next day.

Thank you for your great performance and making our banquet such a success and especially for your kindness to me and my friends.

Sincerely,
James E. Myers
Seminole, Oklahoma

Dear Mr. Clower & Family,

I just finished reading your book, *Ain't God Good!*

I must say it is one of the best books I've read in some time. Yes, God is Good! I gave the book to my husband to read on his way back to Germany where he is stationed.

Now he will find out why I laughed, cried, and said "Amen, Praise God." All at the same time.

He wanted to read it before he left. I said, "No, just wait. This will ease the pain of leaving us behind." Our family consists of three dogs and a darling daughter, age twenty months.

In closing, may God bless you and keep up the good work of God.

The John Joiner Family
El Paso, Texas

LET THE HAMMER DOWN!

Dear Mr. Clower,

Realizing you receive so very many letters, I apologize for taking up your time.

Although I feel you are a great comedian, this is not really a fan letter as such. I simply wanted to write and tell you how my life was changed by reading your book, *Ain't God Good!* I had always been what one might call a marginal Christian. I believed in God and Jesus Christ, but don't ask me to live a life devoted to the way of Christ, was my attitude. I bought your book mainly out of curiosity, took it home and read it in one sitting. Since reading it, nothing in my life has been the same. I look at life through different eyes and I look forward to each day. I'm searching for a church home now, and look forward to making a public confession of faith. God works in mysterious ways, and I truly believe he chose your book to show me the way to life. So, to the title of your book, *Ain't God Good!*, I add, he is indeed. Thank you, Mr. Clower.

Thank you for your time, and may you and yours enjoy life's blessings always.

Sincerely,
David Hansberry
Round Rock, Texas

Dear Jerry,

I just wanted to write and let you know I truly enjoyed your book, *Ain't God Good!* I cried, laughed and got a big blessing out of reading it. I looked for months before I finally found a copy of it in Memphis, Tennessee at the Mid-South Fair. Now I have it loaned all the time, and would you believe I have to keep a list of people wanting it next!

I live between Jonesboro and Blytheville. I don't figure you have ever heard of Leachville. I am a Baptist Sunday School teacher and interpreter for the deaf in Mississippi County. We are the only church of any kind in our county that has services for the deaf and our doors are opened for all services. My husband of fourteen years is deaf. A good Christian man and usher for our church. We have two sons we are very proud of.

Jerry, we are so proud of you. Anyone that will stand up and say he loves the Lord in front of the world is truly a Christian witness. So many people have to tell people they are Christians, but not you Jerry, you live it.

You may never see my letter, but I feel better after writing it. I hope we get your book in our area. Anytime you are ever in Arkansas, please feel free to stop by and see us. You would sure be welcome.

Love in Christ,
Mrs. Jill Poe
Leachville, Arkansas

Dear Jerry,

I have just finished reading your book and it really is inspirational reading material. I hope you and yours had a great Christmas and have a tremendously good 1977.

Your friend,
Jim Carlen
Athletic Director/
Head Football Coach
University of South Carolina

LET THE HAMMER DOWN!

Dear Mr. Clower,

You may never read this letter, but the Lord has convicted me to write anyway.

I have just finished reading *Ain't God Good!*, and praise the Lord you were convicted to write a book. I have never been as touched or as thrilled by any Christian as I have by your book. I believe that we as Christians need to encourage and love each other. And Mr. Clower, you through your life, book and testimony have encouraged me. I feel that you love, even though you have never met people.

I want to tell you that it is really encouraging to see a Christian man who is humble, loving and most of all happy about his salvation.

I want you to know that even though we have never met or probably never will, that my prayers are with you. May God continue to bless you and may He continue to show you the way of the road.

If you could in your schedule find time to write I would really enjoy hearing from you. But even if you don't, I just want to say: Jerry, keep on "Knockin' Out John." Knocking them out for Jesus Christ.

> Your brother in Christ,
> Bob Walker
> Midland, Texas

Dear Jerry,

Just finished reading *Ain't God Good!* and I thoroughly enjoyed every minute!

One thing did trouble me though and I feel led to write you this letter.

As a Christian, I know you emulate Jesus in your everyday life. Jesus was not a "hog" and He doesn't want you to be one either.

You exert so much energy in everything you do . . . that extra weight makes you a prime candidate for a heart attack.

The work you are doing for the Lord is too important for you to jeopardize your health. This old world needs a Jerry Clower.

God has helped you do everything since day one and He can take that fat off you if He wants to and if you will let Him. Jerry, I really do believe He wants you slim. The example you would set for your children would be wonderful. You mentioned that your children had some bad eating habits that needed to be curbed. I was a daddy's youngun' just like your kids are. I always copied what my father did. Especially at the table. If my daddy said it was good, I wanted some. If I had a tendency to gain weight, I wouldn't be able to get through the door, 'cause my daddy was a big eater and I learned to be a big eater from him. I'm very thankful that I've never had a problem with weight, although I may in years to come, and I'm working on cultivating more sensible eating habits.

Jerry, I do hope you read this in the spirit with which it is written. I love you, brother, and thank God for you.

Sincerely,
Jo Ann Nobles
Memphis, Tennessee

P.S. I will pray for you.

LET THE HAMMER DOWN!

Dear Jerry,

I am a housewife from Georgetown, Kentucky with two children and a grandfather to care for. And I just read your book *Ain't God Good!* I have only one thing to say, No, God ain't good, He's Grrrreat. When I first heard people talk about you, I wouldn't listen. I thought anything that funny and pleasing to all those who I knew liked the baser talk records had to be dirty. But as time went by I heard parts of your records and liked them. So when I saw your book in the Kroger store, I bought it. I went back and got three more copies and gave them to friends.

Keep up the good work and keep everyone laughing, and keep on loving God.

> Yours in Christ,
> Patsy Swift
> Georgetown, Kentucky

Dear Mr. Clower,

By pure accident I have just finished reading your book entitled *Ain't God Good!* A friend said to me, "I have a book you probably would like to read since you are from Yazoo City, Mississippi, and it is mentioned a lot of times." I said before I saw it that it was written by Jerry Clower. Sure it was. I did not put it down until I had read two or three chapters.

I enjoyed reading the book for many reasons: I had watched you on TV a little, but there was no way to tell how strong a Christian you professed to be. It was revealed in your book. We share many of the same beliefs about life. Your ideas about rearing children made me think of my father who never promised us anything he did not do. I got every whipping he ever promised me and more too. Today I thank him for every one.

The story of your real father was touching, but the thing that touched me the most, was how you feel about people and especially black people. Jerry, if the white ministers had the strength and backbone to take a stand from the pulpit that you have taken concerning the race issue, we would not have a race problem today. There should not have been a voting about the choir coming to your church because one member was black.

Many whites are going to be disappointed on the day of reckoning when they open their eyes and find that we all are the Lord's children and he loves us equally as much.

Jerry, we are blamed by some whites for not being able to capture the world. But those who blame us should stop and ask themselves: "What have I done to help rather than hinder the plight of blacks?" We have to climb the ladder of success with a double load rather than the normal single load.

You inspired me to do better as a Christian. Yazoo City is my home. I am a brother to Willie (Bill) Brown, Raymond, Robert and many others. My sweet mother Rosie. They live on Wolf Lake, Route 4.

Pray for me and I for you. Your book should be read by everyone and kept along side the Bible.

> Sincerely yours,
> Reaver E. Brown
> Huntsville, Alabama

LET THE HAMMER DOWN!

Dear Mr. Clower,

I just wanted to share with you how buying your book today and reading it had helped change my life.

Being completely sold out for Jesus, I had thought was something to be reserved for preachers, etc. But after reading your book, it finally hit me that that wonderful option is open to anyone—even me!

I just got off my knees from asking Jesus to come in and take completely over. I was saved October 12, 1975, but I never completely sold myself out. Thank God and praise His name, He led me to buy your book and reach this decision.

He may work in strange ways, but He also works in wonderful ways. . . .

Praise His name!

Sincerely,
Mrs. Dale Strachan
Irvington, Alabama

P.S. Your show at the fair in Mobile was wonderful.

14

Who's Country?

My, what a great time I'm having in traveling around all over the country.

In the last 12 months I've done 200 shows. Such wonderful people I have met! There is no more North, South, East, or West in show business. I've often said that I am a country performer. But that doesn't shame me. The reason it doesn't shame me any . . . who is country?

If you see a big TV special, you'll see some folks out of Nashville performing on it. You know over half of the recordings made in the world are made in Nashville. That's where it's at. And I do as many shows· in the North as I do in the South.

Thank God, show business has been used more to stamp out sectionalism, regionalism, racism, and bigotry than any other profession or occupation in the world. Boy, are we making progress!

Because here is a man from south Georgia who apparently wasn't judged by how he talked or what kind of brogue he had or where he was from. But he was looked at as an individual. And people decided whether they thought he had the ability to be President of the United States or not. This is what has happened in show business.

I'm having more fun traveling around all over the country seeing how high society, city folks, is trying to live like I was forced to live years ago. A lot of high society city people I have met in the last few years are trying to buy 'em a little patch of ground out in the country and put 'em a shack on it and run out there every weekend and live like I was forced to live during the Depression. It beats all I've ever seen.

I had the privilege of doing the Theatre in the Round in Boston, Massachusetts, a beautiful place, and I was treated so nice. While in Boston I read in the paper where some thieves broke into a mercantile store. The main thing they were stealing—are you ready for this?— was overalls. Do you hear me?

The young people in Boston, Massachusetts, are wearing overalls. It's the "in" thing, and denim is scarce. At the time I was up there you couldn't buy enough overalls to go around. They were scarce. And if you could steal you a few pair and put them on the black market, you could make a good bit of money.

Why, anybody that grew up country ought to rejoice right here, because they were at least thirty to forty years ahead of their time. Now, city folks, if you grew up in the city, I love you. I fought a war to give you the right to live where you want to live, so don't think I'm picking on you. But if you grew up in the country, just think, you were forty years ahead of your time! Any pants that you owned that weren't overalls, were referred to as dress pants. And here's folks now in this modern day's time, stealing overalls in a big city.

Just think, it took me twenty years just to get out of overalls. I remember the first pair of khaki britches I ever owned. Mama ordered them from Sears and Roebuck. She ordered them from way up North in Memphis, Tennessee. I remember the mail rider, the day he came driving up in that A Model on that dirt road. I was sitting on the side of the road and my heart was beating fast because I was going to have some new khaki britches. That mail rider drove up and handed me that box through the window. I just squatted right in the middle of the dirt road and busted that box open, and there was my new khaki britches. I was feeling so good about them. In fact, I felt so good I wanted to put them on. I just pulled my overalls off and threw them down in the middle of the dirt road. That's all I had on. Mama wouldn't let us wear underclothes with overalls because it would fade on them. That's right. And if you get you a brand new pair of those blue denim overalls in the middle of the hot summer time, they'd blue you up pretty good, too.

Well, I was yelling and hollering and screaming, and down the road I heard a fellow coming and I looked and the dust was boiling up and it was my dear friend Marcel Ledbetter.

"Jerry, what you yelling about?"

"Man, look a here. I got me some new khaki britches."

"Jerry, they're so pretty. You know what we ought to do? The next time old Tarzan is playing on the picture show in town, me and you ought to take us a good bath, and I'll put on the best pair of britches I got and you put on your new khaki britches, and we'll go to town and see old Tarzan."

The mail rider told us that old Tarzan was going to be playing at the local theatre in about three weeks. The local theatre being in McComb, Mississippi.

So the day arrived. Man, we took our bath . . . and

this is another thing I want to interject right here. I read the other day where some big professor was given a plaque—now you country folks listen to this—this big professor was given a testimonial dinner and a plaque due to his beautiful research. He had discovered that the solar system, the sun, could be used to heat water. Yes, think of that.

And forty years ago, me and Marcel Ledbetter drew up a bucket of water and poured the bucket in a number three washtub and set the number three washtub, on a Saturday afternoon, out in the sun, and that night squatted in the tub and bathed ourselves in that good warm water. And forty years later they give some professor a plaque for figuring that out.

Me and Marcel drew up the water on the Saturday that old Tarzan was going to be playing in the town. We squatted in it, bathed ourselves, and I put on my new khaki britches. We got ready to go to the picture show and discovered we didn't have a cent. Not a dime. Aunt Pet Ledbetter, Marcel's mama, gave us a pound of butter. She said, "Now you boys take this pound of butter and hitchhike to town, sell the butter, get you a show ticket, go to the picture show, but you come on home as soon as the show's over because tomorrow is church and Sunday school and we are going."

Me and Marcel hitchhiked to town. Up and down the street, gonna peddle that butter.

Wouldn't nobody buy it. And I commenced to squalling and I sat down on the sidewalk out in front of the picture show and I commenced to crying. Business men would walk by and pat me on top of the head and say, "Don't cry, little boy," but wouldn't none of them give me eleven cents to buy me a show ticket.

About that time Marcel hollered, "Jerry, come on in here. I done sold this pound of butter for twenty-five cents."

I said, "Man, Aunt Pet Ledbetter, your mama, said not to take less than thirty cents a pound for it."

Marcel said, "I can't help it, the music is starting. Old Tarzan is fixing to come out there, and I want to see old Tarzan."

Well, we bought us two show tickets for eleven cents each, rushed into the picture show, bought us three sticks of candy with the three cents left out of the quarter, sat down about halfway back and commenced to chomping on that candy. The lights went out, the curtain parted Metro–Goldwyn–Mayer and that lion said, "AWWWRHHH!" and Marcel Ledbetter jumped up about halfway back and said, "Roar, roar, you scoundrel you. Tarzan will be out there in a minute and tear you up."

While we were there at that picture show, the folks told us that old Tarzan was going to be playing again in ninety days. Ninety days. Marcel said, "Jerry, we got ninety days to raise eleven cents apiece."

So we went back home and got to figuring out a way to get eleven cents apiece so we could see old Tarzan when he came back to the picture show ninety days from then.

Me and Marcel got to praying that cotton would open up early. Yes, it was in the early fall. We just went to school a half a day back in those days when cotton was open, because us young'uns would have to go home at noon and pick cotton 'til dark. And then get up and catch the school bus a little after daylight and go 'til noon again. Some of these folks describing quality education today, I'm glad they didn't have committees to come check my school when I was growing up, because they'd shut our school down. Because we went eight months and we just went a half a day in the fall.

But those of us who wanted to learn, did learn, and we passed college, too, when we got on to college. A little bit too much emphasis is put on what you've got to know before you know anything. Some people are educated beyond their intelligence. I have met a lot of folks with that problem.

Cotton did open up and they were paying four bits a hundred and dinner. Now you folks that ain't cultured enough to understand this, four bits is fifty cents. And if you picked a hundred pounds of cotton for a fellow, he'd give you fifty cents for picking it. And also he'd feed you. Well, I could get 300 pounds a day when I was a young'un. And you know that was a lot of money, because there was a period in my life when I didn't have any money. It was hard to come by.

I remember as a little boy, standing at the 4-H Club roundup at the fairgrounds at Liberty, Mississippi, and I would get off over there and stand by myself, and I'd watch 'em go up to the hamburger stand and buy those hamburgers. Yeah, and I could smell 'em cooking. I wanted one so bad. And folks, I have actually cried as a little old boy because I wanted a hamburger so bad and I couldn't have one. The reason I couldn't have one is very simple. They didn't cost but a nickel, you know. Those nickel ones back then may be better than the dollar ones now. But the reason was real simple that I couldn't buy me a hamburger.

I didn't have a nickel.

But I'll tell you what; it's an ill wind that blows nobody good. While standing barefooted at the Amite County fairgrounds in Liberty, Mississippi, crying because I couldn't have a hamburger because I didn't have a nickel, I looked toward the heavens and I vowed before God, "Oh, Lord, if I ever get in the position to have the money in my pocket and I smell the odor of a hamburger cooking, I'll eat me one."

Hawww! And so help me God, I've been true to that vow ever since.

We picked us some cotton, me and Marcel Ledbetter. We made us some money. We hitchhiked back to town. I wore my new khaki britches. We went to the Taste and Sip hamburger place in McComb, Mississippi. We ate us a hot dog and a hamburger and a RC Cola. You could get a hamburger for a nickel, a hot dog for a nickel, and RC Cola for a nickel. For fifteen cents, you could cut up a town. You could just have a time.

So we got through eating a hamburger, a hot dog, and a RC Cola and we ran up the hill and into the picture show. We bought our show tickets and a great big box of popcorn.

Old Tarzan played again in town and cotton wasn't open. We didn't have any money. The hens weren't laying enough eggs for us to peddle eggs. The cow wasn't giving enough milk for Aunt Pet Ledbetter to churn and give us butter. Marcel said, "Jerry, you know what we ought to do? We ought to get our coon dog and go coon hunting. Catch a bunch of coons and skin 'em and send the hides off to St. Louis. And when that check comes back, man, we'll have us enough money to go to the picture show."

We went coon hunting and caught a bunch of 'em and skinned 'em and dried the hides, sent 'em to St. Louis and waited thirty days, and here came a check. The mail rider brought it. We danced all the way to the house singing, "Gonna get to go see old Tarzan. Gonna see Tarzan, ha, ha, ha. Gonna see Tarzan. Gonna see Tarzan." Ran in the house and mama opened the letter to get the check out of it, and it was for a dime. Ten cents. That's all the money the coon hides brought.

Marcel said, "Jerry, we gonna have to raise twelve more cents, and we ain't got but about sixty more days to do it in. We ought to get our 'possum dog and go 'possum hunting. Let's go over yonder to that persimmon grove, way up yonder northeast of East Fork Consolidated High School and go 'possum hunting, skin and dress them 'possums, and sell fresh dressed 'possum."

"All right, let's go."

We took off, got up there, and commenced to turning the dog loose. Then we heard the train a'coming. The railroad tracks ran through the woods. Whoo! Whoo! Marcel said, "Hold that dog, Jerry. Don't let that dog a–loose." And Marcel Ledbetter took a red bandanna handkerchief and tied it around a coal oil lantern, and it made that coal oil lantern blood red. Marcel ran to the railroad, stood in the middle of the tracks. He put his right foot on one rail, put his left foot on the other rail and faced the oncoming train, and commenced to swinging that lantern.

"Marcel, what are you doing?"

"I'm gonna flag the train."

"You idiot, you gonna get run over."

Marcel was waving that lantern. "Jerry, I'm giving them the distress signal. Oh, man, I'm stopping the train."

About that time, sparks came out from under every wheel. The train came to a stop about twenty feet from Marcel. The engineer and the fireman jumped off the train, ran up to Marcel, and said, "Sir, we saw your distress signal, the red light. Oh, what is the emergency? Is the bridge out?"

"They ain't no emergency. I would just like to know if either one of you gentlemen would like to buy a 'possum."

The engineer looked at him and said, "You idiot. You mean to tell me that you have flagged a hundred-car banana train, refrigerated cars loaded down with bananas, express train from New Orleans to Chicago? Do you mean to tell me you flagged a hundred-car banana train to see if we wanted to buy a dad-blamed 'possum?"

"You want one or not?"

The engineer pulled some money out of his pocket

and said, "Well, I hate for this to be a lost cause. I love 'possum. I just as well buy one inasmuch as you done flagged the train down."

"I ain't caught him yet," Marcel said.

15

The Most Unforgettable People, Places, and Things I've Ever Met

To be truthful, I'd have to call this chapter "*Some* of the Most Unforgettable People, Places and Things I've Ever Met."

Because every day I meet some folks who are hard to forget. These are some of the people I'd like to share with the readers of this book. It's by no means *all* of the most unforgettable I've ever met.

The number one fellow that's hard for me to forget is Tandy C. Rice.

Tandy Rice is my manager. He owns and operates Top Billing, Inc. in Nashville. This young Citadel graduate, on his own energy, enthusiasm, and hard work, owns the agency today that books more Grand Ole Opry stars than any other agency in the world. I met him right after I started easing or backing into show business, but I never really blasted on into it until this man started managing my show business career.

He's almost indescribable. One of the things I'd like to

share with you that would cause you to believe why I think he's one of the most unforgettable people I've ever met is to tell you about how he let the hammer down.

Right after I signed with Top Billing, Tandy caught an airplane and flew to New York City. He went to the Rockefeller Center, the Time Building, and went up to the *Sports Illustrated* department. Then he said, "I'd like to see this editor named Robert W. Creamer."

"Well, Mr. Creamer is pretty busy," they said.

"I know it. Anybody that's worth anything, that's doing a good job, is busy. I am willing to wait to see that dear man."

It came time for Tandy to go in to see him and the reason he wanted to see him was he wanted *Sports Illustrated* to do a feature story on Jerry Clower from Yazoo City, Mississippi.

"Why?" the man asked.

"Well, the first college football game Jerry Clower ever saw, he played in it. He does some banquets for universities and colleges, football banquets, and all–awards sports banquets, and things like that, and he is a good fellow and an athletic devotee. I mean, he loves sports, keeps up with it all the time, and I know he'd be a great subject for an article in *Sports Illustrated*."

Now, people, Mr. Creamer, the editor, stopped Tandy Rice: "Wait just a minute, sir."

He pushed a button, called in his secretary, and said to her, "Bring in all the employees who work for *Sports Illustrated*. Bring them into my office; stand 'em up in here; I want to tell them something."

They all gathered in his office. Mr. Creamer got up and said, "Ladies and gentlemen, I want to show you an illustration of dedication and believing in your product. I want you to listen to the presentation this man is making to me. Mr. Rice, you start all over. I want all of these people to hear the presentation you made to me about

Jerry Clower and why we ought to do an article on him."

Tandy said it again.

"You have your article," the editor told him. "Mr. Roy Blount, Jr., you work it out."

Ladies and gentlemen, Roy Blount, Jr.—a great writer—came to Yazoo City, Mississippi, and just lived with me for a week. If I went to do a show, he'd catch the same plane. He slept in my boy's bedroom. And April 30, 1973, he did an eight-page spread on Jerry Clower.

In my opinion, that was the main springboard for me to receive national recognition—inasmuch as phones started ringing even from Canada and from all over the United States wanting to know more about this Jerry Clower.

Yes, Tandy Rice is one of the most unforgettable people I've ever met. This is just one illustration of why I have to put him in a book that's titled, *Let the Hammer Down.*

The next individual is Paul Moyer.

In 1957 and 1958, I lived in what's known as the Home Seeker's Paradise, Brookhaven, Mississippi. That's where I created one of the dearest friends a human being could be allowed to have in Alcus Smith. (I covered Alcus very thoroughly in my first book, *Ain't God Good!*)

Paul Moyer was the high school football coach. On that team he had Lance Alworth, Ralph "Catfish" Smith, and many other outstanding young men. He led them to unbelievable heights in football.

Paul Moyer was a buddy of mine. He was an easygoing fellow, successful, and he was later promoted to Athletic Director.

One time one of his running backs quit, and the young man was mixed up. I went to see the young man, counseled with him, and said, "Son, you're making a mistake. You have all the ability in the world to get you a college scholarship. Your folks can't afford to send you to school. Why don't you reconsider?"

"I don't know whether Coach Moyer would let me come back or not."

"Will you allow me to take you to Coach Moyer? Just me and you and him? He's interested in young people. Let's see if we can work out something."

We drove up in Paul Moyer's front yard, and Paul and I and this young boy counseled and talked. Paul agreed to let him face the squad and apologize.

It was handled so beautifully. He salvaged a young man who came back and played football.

But the most unforgettable thing about Paul Moyer was his spirit when cancer entered his body and he started deteriorating. He slowed down.

The Touchdown Club of Brookhaven, a very active, energetic group that really pushes sports for Brookhaven public schools, had a Paul Moyer Day. And Paul Moyer, after this day, wrote a letter to the Touchdown Club members.

He was a man's man, and recreated here. I want you to read this letter that Paul Moyer, the Athletic Director, wrote on November 15, 1971, to the Touchdown Club members just before he went home to be with the Lord.

Dear Fellow Touchdown Members,

"Paul Moyer Day" was, of course, one of the biggest thrills and greatest honors any man could ever receive, and I am truly grateful for it. This has made me feel very humble and undeserving of all this honor and attention.

To each of you let me say a special "thank you," because without your help I could not have carried out any of my projects or any of the other small accomplishments which might be attributed to me. Each and every time I came before you with one of my crazy ideas about a project, you were ready, not only to do what I ask, but to go way beyond in cooperating in every possible way: money, labor, supplies, and of course your confidence and encouragement.

But just let me, in football terminology, tell you how we stand right now on our latest project. First of all, thanks to each and every one of you who has joined my team in this game of "Life vs. Cancer." I'll tell you, this is about the toughest opponent I've ever run into, but you know there has never been a team yet that could not be beaten at a certain time with the right opponent. And with all of you on my team I believe we can offer some pretty good opposition.

However, in the eventuality that we don't win this one, because you know, "You can't win them all," I am prepared to walk off the field, knowing that we have fought a good fight, with my hand in the hand of the greatest coach of all times, "The Coach from Nazareth."

So you see, team, we really can't lose either way, can we? Let's all just keep our chins up, dig in, and keep fighting. "We've been in tighter places than this before."

Sincerely,
Paul Moyer, Athletic Director

Now after reading this letter, can't you see why I would include Paul Moyer among the most unforgettable people I've ever met? If there was ever a man who under God wanted to *Let the Hammer Down,* Paul let it down.

Paul Moyer. God rest his beautiful soul.

Friends, this is what it's all about. This book could have been named *Let the Hammer Down with Laughter* or *Let the Hammer Down While Living* because this is how to live.

Here's a man who said, "Look, I'm gonna fight this thing, and I'm prepared to whoop up on it, but eventually, if I don't win this one, I'll take a-hold of the hand of the coach from Nazareth."

And that's the way it is! Let me move on. The Lord may come while I'm talking about Paul Moyer.

One of the most unforgettable people I've ever met is Reverend Aubrey Smith.

While I was living in Yazoo City a few years ago, the Methodist Bishop sent a young preacher to Yazoo City to be pastor of the First United Methodist Church. His name was Aubrey Smith.

My, what a man!

He would come as near saying the right thing at the right time of any man I've ever known in my life.

The part of his life that causes me to be unable to forget him was during the period he was pastor of the First Methodist Church.

The First Baptist Church of Yazoo City, my church, was without a pastor. We had a good pulpit committee, and they were looking for another man to be our spiritual leader. But it took eight months to find the leadership of the Lord in finding the man who ought to be pastor of our church. Thank God, the Lord led them to Brother Jim Yates—a man I love with every fiber of my being, and a man who has been my pastor for the last fifteen years of my life.

While we were without a pastor during these eight months, Aubrey Smith, the pastor of the Methodist church, visited all of our sick. He'd get a list of the sick folks in the hospital and would visit all the Baptists and explain to them, "Until you get you a preacher now, Brother Aubrey will be right here with you. I want you to know I'm at your side."

One day I saw Brother Aubrey and he had mud all over his shoes and red clay dirt on the britches legs of his beautiful suit.

"Brother Aubrey, where in the world have you been?" I asked.

"I've been up in north Mississippi burying the mother of one of your deacons. One of your fine Baptist deacons' mother died and, as you know, you don't have a pastor, so I've been up in north Mississippi conducting a burial service for this deacon's mama."

My, how impressive! This is the way God wants it done, in my opinion.

Thank God, Aubrey Smith has shown other folks how it ought to be done.

I've seen ministerial associations in a town squabble. The Baptist couldn't get along with the Catholic fellow, or the Catholic fellow couldn't get along with the Presbyterian fellow, especially when you were having a liquor election, whether you were for it or against it. But Aubrey Smith conducted himself as a man of God.

While I was having the privilege of being chairman of the pulpit supply committee, I suggested to our group that we invite Brother Aubrey to preach in the First Baptist Church one Sunday night. I contacted him and he said, "Sure, we'll have early service in the United Methodist Church, and we'll get out in time to come over and I'll preach for you all."

The choir loft was full of folks. Brother Aubrey was

coming. The Methodist preacher what loved us enough to pray with us and to bury our dead.

He was coming over here to preach for us. He got up there that night—I'll never forget it—and preached about the rich young ruler. And he said, "What must I do to be saved?" He gave an invitation.

At the close of the service, he explained to all the people present there that night, "I know some of you are awaiting baptism, and you may have a conviction you want to be baptized soon, and you don't want to wait for your pastor to come. If you have this conviction, you all run some water in that baptistry—Brother Smith knows how to do it—and I'll be glad to do it for you."

Yes, here is a man, Reverend Aubrey Smith. He stayed in Yazoo City some eight or nine years. I remember when they transferred him. The Bishop was led by the Lord to move him out of this town.

I cried. I sat down and squalled like a baby because a man of God was leaving town. Reverend Aubrey Smith —one of the most unforgettable people I've ever met, and a real preacher who the Lord used to let the hammer down.

A. B. Kelly and his wife, Dorothy. Two of the most unforgettable people I've ever met.

Thank God, I have the privilege of rubbing elbows with them now, because every time I go to church they're there.

A. B. Kelly is my life insurance agent. I've known him since 1954, and I'm not remembering him due to his expertise in being a life insurance agent, even though I might be the biggest customer he's got. But I remember

him as being a man, and the main thing I can't forget
about A. B. and Dorothy Kelly is their attitude.

Awww, people! All of you who want to do the best
you can with what you've got (which I've defined here
as letting the hammer down), you've got to have the
right kind of attitude.

In fact, attitude could be more important than facts.
That's right. If David had listened to the facts, he never
would have fought Goliath. Never in ever would he
have fought Goliath if he had of listened to the facts.
But he had the right attitude.

Years ago the First Baptist Church of Yazoo City was
located downtown close to the courthouse. We were
having two services every Sunday morning because the
church was so small that we had more folks than we
could get in there. We were also having one service on
Sunday night.

A group of people in the church suggested that we
buy a lot out on Grand Avenue. A big lot. Sell our
downtown property and build from the ground up out
on Grand Avenue.

Whoooo!, some folks opposed this! They felt strong
about not moving that church. If we were going to re-
build, let's do it right here. Tear the wall out or try to do
something. There was a strong feeling that the church
ought to stay where it was and not move it to the bigger
lot out on Grand Avenue.

A.B. and Dorothy felt as strong about not moving
that church as anybody in the First Baptist Church of
Yazoo City. First time it was brought up, it was voted
down. Second time it was brought up, it was voted down.
The third time it was brought up, the deacons recommended it, but A.B. Kelly made a minority report on
behalf of some of the deacons that he was against it.

We had the final vote on a Sunday night. We stayed
there several hours. A.B. and Dorothy expressed them-

selves real strong that they didn't want to move it. The vote was this time—after three tries—that we were going to move the church and build a brand new one.

Well, right off, I said A.B. and Dorothy feel so strong about this, they'll probably join another church. They won't go out there.

But the thing I remember the most about them and others who believed as they did was that on the day we cut the ribbon for the beautiful, new church—all spacious and beautiful from the ground up, bricks and splendor—the day we cut the ribbon, two of the most smiling, beaming, handshaking folks I saw there that day were A.B. and Dorothy Kelly: Welcome, come on into *our* new church. *Our* new church!

My, what an attitude they showed!

They illustrate how Christians ought to let the hammer down about attitudes. Yes, A.B. Kelly and Dorothy Kelly are two of the most unforgettable people I've ever met.

In my first book, I listed some of my closest friends, and mentioned that my closest friend was Charles J. Jackson. I must also list him as one of the most unforgettable people I've ever met.

Charles J. Jackson does have a genuine zest for living and doesn't try to appear to be anything but himself twenty-four hours a day. And I love him.

You know in this big world of executives and pushing and pulling and briefcases and "I don't have time to do this" and "I'm just overworked," they even do commercials now on television about how to rent a car, showing a fellow running to get to his plane. Anybody that ain't no more organized than that ought not be an executive. Unless you had a wreck or a flat tire, you are unorganized.

Some executives I know almost miss the plane because they can't walk by a telephone. They think of somebody they need to call. All the time they didn't need to call anybody. It was just a waste of time.

I've been right in the middle of a commercial, I mean laying it down good, and some fellow was called to the telephone. And they talked, and it wasn't any more necessary than them flying to the moon.

Charles J. Jackson is a living illustration of a top flight executive who's loved by everybody who works for him, that gets the job done and works for the finest company ever built anywhere in the world. And he's my dear friend.

Charles J. Jackson is one of the most unforgettable people I've ever met, and he lets the hammer down in every phase of his life.

He taught me how to give.

He's the most humanitarian man I've ever known.

Folks in the county—a lot of them poverty–stricken— call him more than they do the welfare department, because he has a compassionate heart, and he knows how to get it on. He doesn't own a briefcase. To my knowledge, he's never made a phone call after office hours, and he runs a giant empire.

He knows more before breakfast about how to get along with people than most other folks will know the rest of their lives.

My, how I wish Charles J. Jackson could rub off on other people where they could get 'em a little slower gait and go through life having a fun time living and enjoying their work, making life pleasant for people they work with. So, my friend Charles J. Jackson is one of the most unforgettable people I've ever met.

Another reason I love Charles Jackson is that he's a

civic–minded individual. How I love him for being interested in the community in which he lives, and trying to better it. He's been president of the Chamber of Commerce and the Rotary Club and so forth. He's been a city councilman and serves the city as one of the city fathers.

He's a living illustration of my theme—there's no limit to what can be done if it doesn't matter who gets the credit.

I love him because he works for his city during a time when one of the bad problems in this country is that there are folks among us that if you tore down the entire city they live in and didn't leave anything standing except where they work and where they live, they wouldn't notice it. And it bothers me.

We've got some folks in my own hometown who are rich and wealthy who don't take part in doing anything. Not anything. They may come out of their routine of making money every day if they can stop something they don't like. It may not even be good for the town, but they'll come out and stop that. And, my soul, get it on, Brother Jackson! I hope you live to be a thousand years old.

Next most unforgettable person I've ever met is Raymond Lindsey.

I'm a member of Gideons International—an association of Christian business and professional men who have banded themselves together to win men and women, boys and girls to the Lord Jesus Christ.

This is the only objective this fine association has. One of the ways they reach this objective is by placing the Word of God in national streams of life all over the world. They've done a fantastic work for the Lord since the Gideons was started years and years ago.

Raymond Lindsey was a very active Gideon who lived in Little Rock, Arkansas. Back in the early days of the Gideons being started in Mississippi, we needed some guidance. So we asked some Gideons from other states to come to Mississippi to help us.

One of the very important things that the Gideons International does is to place testaments in the hands of school children from the fifth through the twelfth grades. This is voluntary.

We go into the schools; we offer the testaments. The Gideons do not preach. They just simply say, "Here is the Word of God. It's made possible by contributions from local churches, and we've purchased these testaments. They're absolutely free to you. All we ask you to do is read it, and if you'd like one, would you please come by and take the testament out of our hand."

It's voluntary on the part of the school children if they'd like to have a testament. This is a beautiful testament. It also includes Psalms and Proverbs.

The Gideons International goes to the fifth through the twelfth grades, as I mentioned, and each year they go back to the fifth grade. That way, each and every child in the schools can have one if he or she deserves one.

The Gideons hadn't been too active in Mississippi for some time, and we were meeting in Greenville for the first distribution of Bibles ever attempted in Mississippi. The Bibles would be placed on the teacher's desk, and the testaments would be given to the school children.

We all got to Greenville, and the school board voted that this task could not be done. We did our best to notify the Gideons from Little Rock not to come, but they had already left home.

When they got there, Raymond Lindsey did a thing under God that causes me to name him as one of the most unforgettable people I have ever met. It also gives one of the most beautiful testimonies for prayer which I believe in very strongly with every fiber of my being.

To get this story accurate, I contacted one of my dear friends that I love very much—Brother G.W. Blankenship, a Gideon who is retired in Little Rock. I said, "Brother Blankenship, let's you and me talk about that beautiful moment when Raymond Lindsey and you and some others showed up at Greenville, Mississippi, with the Greenville Gideons and some Gideons throughout the state. Let's talk about what happened when Raymond Lindsey, a man of God, led our group to literally call on God to help us."

Here's that remarkable story direct from a man directly involved in it, G.W. Blankenship:

"Jerry, I'll give you the account of Greenville's great victory for Christ, when the Gideons made the first distribution of Bibles ever attempted in Mississippi.

"My own part in this event is of minor importance. It occurred about thirty years ago when the late Raymond Lindsey of Little Rock and myself were both fairly new members of the Gideons International. Even then we had made many school presentations and, of course, many hotel and motel demands were prayerfully answered and supplied.

"The new Gideons of Greenville, as you remember, had never made a Bible presentation in the public schools. This was a task all of us enjoyed, and when the Gideons of Little Rock were asked to help the new group in the dedication of thousands of Bibles for thousands of children in open assembly next morning, we were ready to go.

"I had a phone call at 10 o'clock on Tuesday, the day before the distribution. It was from Raymond Lindsey, the president of the Little Rock Gideons, asking me to accompany three of our group to Greenville, and help arrange the distribution plans. The three who accompanied Raymond Lindsey on this journey to Greenville were Bill Brawner, Clyde Hollis, and myself. All of these men have long since agreed it was the most amazing journey of our lives, for on this occasion we discovered the full possibility of a life that was surrendered to Christ.

"We arrived in Greenville in the afternoon and were greeted by a committee of Mississippi Gideons. They were the most unhappy group alive, and they made no effort to conceal it. They had tried to contact us on our way to Greenville but could make no connection. Simply stated, they had been advised that the school board had met in the morning and had ruled that placing Bibles or any kind of religious literature in the tax paid schools was not in the public interest and was forbidden.

" 'Sorry you had to come on this long trip,' they said, 'but we never thought this would happen. But what will we do with all these Bibles? There are thousands of them and they are all paid for. They said their decision was final. It was unanimous—there is no need to proceed further.'

"Back at the hotel, Raymond Lindsey registered for all of our group as though nothing had happened. 'We came here to distribute the Word of God,' said Raymond. 'And that's what we are going to do.'

"The hotel provided us with a large room with three beds and brought in several chairs. In the room were many of the Greenville men who came to console us and offer words of sorrow and sympathy, but these men needed more than advice.

"Raymond wasted no time in criticizing the citizens of Greenville or the school board. He arranged the chairs in the hotel room and bluntly stated that we were going to have a prayer service. No one was to pray who doubted the power of God to perform miracles! He was in tears when he made this appeal. He was deeply con-

cerned; he cried like a child. We all felt the presence of
God. There were no dry eyes in that room. In all of his
great prayer life did he ever offer such an appeal to God!

"Then Bill Brawner offered a prayer that was start-
ling! This great man of God did not deal in trivialities.
He suddenly cried out, "Oh, Lord! Let those who voted
to deny the Word of God to the children of Greenville
have no sleep until they have changed their minds and
their votes . . . but change their minds tonight . . .
tomorrow will be too late, too late!'

"Clyde Hollis spoke of this prayer meeting the rest of
his life. Imagine someone asking God to withhold sleep
from people who didn't think as you do!

"Raymond Lindsey, who was elected president of
Gideons International some years later, was reminded of
what happened later that night. Many of the men re-
mained for some time after this, but none of us ever
forgot it!

"Raymond glanced at the clock on the wall. It was
getting very late. On a shelf beside the clock was a telephone. It was an old timer and rang loudly when used.

"Raymond moved a large chair into the center of the
room, made it face the clock on the wall, folded his arms,
made himself perfectly at ease, and with a look of perfect
composure, he confided in God. 'I am looking at the
clock, Lord, and I shall not stop praying, nor will I rest
or sleep until that telephone rings. Not until someone
calls over that phone and tells me that the school board
has changed its mind and has granted us permission to
distribute the Word of God in the schools tomorrow!
It's in your hands, Lord. I await your word.'

"That was the trying time of our very lives. The clock
moved on and on. Sleep was forgotten. Every mind was
alert and every eye was on the clock. No one spoke. One
man slowly arose and tiptoed out. No one noticed! The
rest of us watched the phone . . . and then we sat bolt

upright. It was well past 12 o'clock, but the telephone was ringing sharply! Raymond was on his feet in an instant. What was all the excitement about? The phone ringing need cause no excitement! Phones ring day and night!

"It was all over in a few moments!

"With no trace of excitement on his face, Raymond Lindsey had kept his appointment with God. And God had sent some messenger to calmly notify us to go ahead with our distribution. We fell to our knees and praised God again!

"But on our way back to Little Rock, Clyde Hollis spoke for all of us. We stopped for a few words of thanks to God. Imagine God being asked by us to delay the sleep of anyone until his work is finished.

"Some years ago I was addressing the Hamilton Moses Bible Class in Immanuel Baptist Church when Raymond Lindsey slipped in and sat before me. I brought up that unbelievable event. And do you know what he said? 'I had almost forgotten about it,' Raymond Lindsey said simply."

Now is that letting the hammer down or not? It's so beautiful—and I remember it just like Brother Blankenship recalls it.

Raymond Lindsey has gone home to his reward. Praise God, how I look forward to dying because I'm gonna get to fellowship with my dear friend Raymond Lindsey and other friends who believed like he believed, because he had received God's plan of salvation, knew what it meant, and is at home in glory right now.

How I look forward to joining Raymond Lindsey when breath leaves this mortal body of Jerry Clower!

Let me throw in one of the most unforgettable cities I've ever met: Jackson, Mississippi.

The finest city of its size in the world is Jackson. If you ask me to pick out a town that I had to go to in raising some money for a worthy cause, I'd say send me to Jackson.

I'd call on people there like Warren Hood—and Mr. Warren Hood would make a sizeable contribution to any worthwhile cause if I went to him and asked him, because he's one of the people who loves the town and tries to help it progress.

As I travel around all over this world, people tell me, "Yazoo City—that ain't too far from Jackson. I love Jackson—I get to go there some."

Jackson impresses me as being the type of town that ought to be a typical town in America.

After I called on Warren Hood, I'd get him to go with me to see a fellow named Leland Speed. Leland would then go with us and we'd call on some other folks, and it wouldn't be long before we'd have all the money we needed for the cause we were raising the money for. Then I'd go see a fellow named Toby Towbridge. Toby is one of the most unforgettable people I've ever met in the most unforgettable town I know of.

When I get off an airplane at the lovely Jackson Airport, I walk out one of those big beautiful snouts that connects the plane directly to the terminal. Now, when I land in the big, beautiful fun city that you hear about all the time—up there at La Guardia Airport—you walk down a little ladder and get off on the ground and walk through the rain, slush, and snow to get into the airport. This is in the big, fine, Eastern, Northern town that's so up in the world and has so many fine facilities.

But in Jackson, you get off the plane in one of those snouts where the rain and wind can't hit you. That's Jackson Airport—one of the finest airports and terminal facilities for a town that size in the world.

It's also the capital city of my beautiful state of Mississippi.

Recently at the airport, I ran into Toby Towbridge, who's an automobile dealer. He's a happy–go–lucky fellow, and was smiling, hollering, whooping, and clowning with me. He was out there putting a friend on an airplane—a very fine looking gentleman. Just before we went to get on the airplane, Toby whispered to me, "Jerry, somehow or another, I need to talk to you privately."

The man with Toby stayed with him until they boarded. I watched Toby tell him good–by and I stuck around until Toby came up to me.

"Jerry, while you're on that airplane, I want you to go back there and visit with my friend. He's on his way to Houston, Texas, and he's a neighbor of mine. He's a very good doctor here in Jackson, and he's on his way to the M.D. Anderson Cancer Clinic in Houston. He's got cancer, he's been out there a few times, and he's going out there now for some treatments. While you're on that plane I want you to get to know him and talk to him."

And this giant of a man—this happy–go–lucky fellow—looked me right in the eye and he started squalling. He couldn't control his emotions. He cried, "That man is a friend of mine."

I grabbed old Toby and said, "Praise God, there ain't many folks in the world who have got a friend."

"Jerry, I ain't kin to him. He's just my friend and I love him."

How beautiful. That took place in Jackson, Mississippi, with the folks who make up that fine town. So I'll hereby declare that Jackson is the most unforgettable town its size I've ever been in since I've been living in this old world.

Mel Tillis. I don't know why Mel and I got to be so close. He grew up in Florida—poor, like I did.

I've never brought up anything that had to do with country that he couldn't take up the conversation and get right in on it.

I've often had the privilege of doing shows with him like when I do the Mel Tillis shows as his special guest star. I go out and start off the show, about forty to forty-five minutes, and then Mel and his band will come onstage and close the show. But I've never done a show with Mel Tillis that at the end of it he didn't on his last number say, "Ladies and gentlemen, let's get the nation's number one country comic back out here on stage and let you applaud him again. Jerry, would you like to sing this last song with us and stay out here with us?"

Now that's class. Mel Tillis.

The last time I did a show with Mel, I drew me one of those standing ovations up there in Rockford, Illinois. They stood up, hollered, and whooped. Some performers wouldn't have wanted my name brought up again during the whole show. But not Mel Tillis. He said, "Bring ol' Jerry back out here—I want you to applaud him one more time."

Would you believe that while Mel and I were doing some Purina Dog Chow commercials together that here comes a letter from two big national television networks saying that if Mel Tillis stuttered, they wouldn't play the commercials on national television?

You people reading this probably don't believe this happened in this fine, tolerant world we live in. These big networks always claim they set the example against bigotry and racism and discrimination. I'm sure you don't believe the letters were written—but they were.

I want the world to know that we worked two full days on trying to do two commercials in which he would not stutter, so they would be accepted by the two big networks.

Do you hear me?

And we finally did it.

I don't know whether they are going to play them or not, but I want to make it perfectly clear right here what my attitude was: I said a mistake was made. That's just like telling Ronnie Milsap he can't be on national television because he's blind. Or telling Ray Charles the same thing.

These commercials might have been played by the time this book comes out. But the damage was done. I think some young lawyer who didn't know what he was doing up and wrote a letter. In fact, if Mel Tillis can get control of the letters, he can own the network.

It upset Mel. It really did; it bothered him. Here's a young man who's been stuttering since he was three years of age—and here's two big networks that wrote a letter saying, "Son, we won't play your commercials if you stutter."

Isn't that silly?

I still believe it was all a mistake. I don't believe the management of any television network in America—if they knew who Mel Tillis was and knew that he stutters—wouldn't say, "Do your commercials, more power to you, and I'm glad you've made millions of dollars singing and haven't let this speech impediment be a handicap to you."

So, Mel Tillis would be one of the most unforgettable people I've ever met. He's good; he's nice; he's friendly. He's the type of fellow that I'd call in the middle of the night and say, "Melvin."

And he'd say, "What is it?"

And I'd say, "I need you."

He'd say, "All right, Jerry, where are you? I'll come to you, son, and help you if I can."

Now please note, I've got a lot of buddies in show business, a lot of friends in this business. In fact, the rest of this book could just be their names—and I praise God for their friendship. I made it clear at the outset of this chapter that this is some—just *some*—of the most unforgettable people I've met. But I have to put Mel Tillis in that category of one of the most unforgettable people I've ever met. He does the best he can with what he's got, and he gives it a maximum effort. That's my definition of letting the hammer down.

When I was growing up at Route 4, Liberty, Mississippi, there was a black lady who lived there affectionately called Aunt Corindi. Corindi Lacken.

I've seen Aunt Corindi a lot of times, and she'd always give me some advice. She was a devout Christian, and the main thing she knew about God was what she had experienced in her own heart and life. She couldn't read too well, but, my, what a saint she was when it came to knowing about how to love God!

One day she was at my house helping my mother iron. We were talking about several things going on in the community and things we had heard about on the radio. My mother referred to it as meanness: "Too much meanness going on in the world."

Aunt Corindi turned that iron up, put it down on a little piece of metal she had there to keep it from burning the ironing board, looked up at the heavens and said, "Miss Mabel, the devil he is mighty, but the Lord he is *all*mighty."

Praise God, educated folks, all of you good people teaching in the seminaries, come up with a greater, more profound, more beautiful statement than that!

Yes, Aunt Corindi Lacken—I must remember her as

being one of the most unforgettable people I've ever met
because you can't improve on the statement: "The devil
he is mighty, but the Lord He is *all*mighty."

When I came home from the service or college, I'd
see her and ask, "Aunt Corindi, how is so and so doing?"

"I don't know."

"Well, what do you think about the weather?"

"I don't know."

"Have you planted your garden?"

"I haven't planted my garden."

Most of her answers would be "I don't know."

One time I asked her, "Aunt Corindi, how are you and
the Lord getting along?"

"Now then, you have done asked me something I
know something about."

And she'd give a beautiful testimony about the Lord
and what he meant to her.

Jim Ed Brown. Would you believe I've done more
than sixty-five television shows, all of them out on the
road with Jim Ed Brown? That's a bunch of shows.

In doing the weekly television show, "Nashville on
the Road," I never remember at any time under any circumstances—even when the equipment wouldn't func-
tion, the sun went behind a cloud, we had been there all
day long, we were trying to get a show back on schedule, sometimes even at 2:30 or 3 o'clock in the morning
and we had been going all day and all night and really
pushing because the pressure was on us . . . I can never
remember a time under any circumstance when Jim Ed
Brown and I ever had a cross word.

My soul, Jim Ed Brown comes from Arkansas, comes
from good stock. I love him and his sisters—Maxine and
Bonnie—for inventing the Browns' Sound. You heard

it in songs like "The Old Lamplighter," "Scarlet Ribbons," and "Little Jimmy Brown."

As I look back on my show business career, I'd have to say that Jim Ed Brown is one of the most unforgettable people I've ever met. And I love him.

Not only did Jim Ed give the world the Browns' Sound, but now he has a young lady with him, Helen Cornelius. I respect and love her for teaching a class of young people in the First Baptist Church of Hannibal, Missouri. Helen and Jim Ed found the right song, recorded it, and the song became a number one hit on Billboard, Cash Box, and Record World.

It's a joy to work with her, and I thank God that Jim Ed Brown continues creating and keeps adding each year more sounds for the enjoyment of people all over the country.

In this chapter about the most unforgettable people I've ever met, I don't want to indicate that all of them are good people. Thank God, the ones I've mentioned so far are all great folks.

But I have met some folks that I remember not because of their good attitudes, not because of their love of the Lord, not because they love this country and believe in giving an honest day's work for an honest day's pay, but I remember them because their attitude was bad and they were griping and whooping and going on all the time. They were complaining all the time, and nothing pleased them. I won't name any of them by name here.

Attitude. That's the primary thing that makes me remember folks.

Many times when I'm traveling, I rent cars. I recently changed my car rental company because so often I'd get ready to rent a car from these folks, and they may have had 200 cars on their lot, but I'd look better walking or toting one of their cars than I would riding in them.

All of them were little bitty old cars. So I switched around a little bit and then I decided I'd go back to the old folks I'd been renting the cars from.

After renting a car in a Southern town, I was going to drop it off in another town one Sunday morning. I drove up to the place, put the rent–a–car in the parking lot, walked into the big beautiful terminal, up to the counter, put the keys and the papers down on the counter and said, "Good morning."

The lady working for the rent–a–car agency said, "Ain't nothing good about this morning."

"Darling, it's Sunday morning, the sun is shining, I am alive, and I just assumed that would make it a good morning."

"There ain't nothing good about this morning because I have to work."

"Well, darling, lots of people ain't got no jobs, and you ought to give thanks for having a job."

"They wouldn't want this one."

She said it just as hateful as she could.

"Well, lady, why don't you quit and give up this job, and let somebody that wants it and appreciates it have it?"

"Wouldn't nobody want the job, and they wouldn't want it if they had to work on a Sunday."

"I know a lot of folks that wish they had this job." So I figured that I'd better hush. I was trying to help her attitude a little bit, especially knowing that whoever she was working for was probably at home thinking that his rent–a–car service was being operated in a good business-like manner. Run by somebody with a good attitude.

So when she handed me the final papers, I said, "Well,

bye bye, young lady. I sure hope your attitude improves."

She drew back and threw those car keys the length of that counter and hit the wall on the other side.

I went on to my flight praying, "Lord, let her realize what makes this country great. Free enterprise. Folks working. Giving an honest day's work for an honest day's pay."

Unfortunately, this young lady is one of the most unforgettable people I've ever met. I don't want to identify her because I feel sorry for her and I pray for her. The thing that made it so tragic was that she was so pretty. She was just beautiful. If she had just acted like my mama used to tell me. When me and my brother Sonny would get ready to go out on a date, she'd say, "Boys, if you'll act as nice as you look, you'll make out fine."

If that young lady had just acted as nice as she looked, she would have made out fine.

As I got on the airplane, I told myself, "I ain't never gonna rent another car from those people." But I got to thinking, why should I hold that against a company that's in business to serve folks and to make a profit? Her boss might have been on his way to church and Sunday school with his family, thinking that she was doing a good job down there running that counter.

Attitude! It's more important than facts. Because—let me reiterate—little David would have never fought Goliath if he had listened to the facts.

The radio show "Country Crossroads" is heard by millions of people every week all over the world. I certainly enjoy doing this show. I have the privilege of co-hosting this show with Bill Mack, the WBAP—Fort Worth deejay, who is nationally known, especially by truckers all over the nation, and Leroy Van Dyke, a very fine entertainer.

I enjoy being on the show with both of these gentlemen every week. The two people I'm involved with most for the Southern Baptist Convention Radio and Television Commission—that sponsors and puts on this show—are Jim Rupe, the producer, and Stan Knowles, the associate producer.

Jim Rupe is one of the most unforgettable people I've ever met because of his fantastic talent. Not only is he a devout Christian with a beautiful attitude, but he's an instrument rated pilot, and he flies me on occasion.

Jim is an expert scuba diver. As a producer of "Country Crossroads," he can splice and re-dub and do-dub and edit and interview folks and do a fantastic job with the tape that we lay down when we do our part of the show. He's a good family man, just beautiful to work with, and he certainly is one of the most beautiful people I've ever met.

And Stan Knowles. He's an old sweet boy, good to everybody. I saw him not too long ago and he was limping. He hurt his foot helping somebody move something out of their house.

Stan always has somebody in mind that he's trying to help, praying with them, and helping them with their problems. He's one of the most accommodating fellows I've ever known in my life.

So as I name off the people—the most unforgettable ones I've met—I'll have to mention Jim Rupe and Stan Knowles, each living in Fort Worth, Texas, and employed by the Southern Baptist Convention Radio and Television Commission.

I'm so proud of that commission; it makes me praise God to be a Christian and to be associated with a denomination that would have in their sphere of things a fine commission like this that has numerous shows. Millions of people hear the good news and also enjoy a fine program due to the Radio and Television Commission of the Southern Baptist Convention.

Jim Rupe and Stan Knowles . . . two of the most unforgettable people I've ever met.

The next most unforgettable person I've ever met is Jimmy Carter.

Now folks, don't think I'm trying to lead you to believe that President Jimmy Carter is a close personal friend of mine.

He is not. Or hasn't been up until the time of me writing this book. I do know him because I had the privilege of making an appearance on the same platform with him—and he's one of those unforgettable characters.

Jimmy Carter was governor of Georgia at the time. He was invited to speak to the same group that I was. The group was the Congress of the Laity sponsored by Howard E. Butt, Jr., president of the Laity Lodge Foundation. Butt is a millionaire groceryman from Corpus Christi, Texas, an outstanding Baptist layman and director of various Christian organizations, one of them being the Congress of the Laity.

They asked me to attend one of these meetings at the Hyatt Regency in Atlanta. On the program was Jerry Clower, Christian entertainer, member of the Grand Ole Opry, and Jimmy Carter, the governor of Georgia.

When I heard that man's testimony, I was amazed and thrilled. I came back home telling my family how wonderful it was to hear an individual who had been elected to a major political office who was a Christian and wasn't ashamed to say so.

I fellowshiped with Jimmy Carter and got to know him there.

Years ago, in my fertilizer–selling days, I had the good fortune to speak to the Peanut Warehousemen's Association in Savannah, Georgia, and Billy Carter was there and I got to meet him.

Jimmy Carter. Then governor, and now president. To have his deep Christian convictions and then go on with that bulldog, hang–on–foreverishness and accomplish a goal that he set out to accomplish, despite all odds, he's an unforgettable individual.

I had a sweet Christian fellowship with him. I'll never forget it as long as I live—and I'm thrilled that I had the privilege of knowing him and of being for him before he was ever elected as President of the United States.

At the end of a show in Albany, Georgia, I was up on stage and, since we had plenty of time, I opened it up for questions from the audience. Somebody asked me what I thought about Jimmy Carter. "Well, anybody that's got enough common sense to be versed in nuclear physics and still have enough common sense to grow peanuts has got to be my kind of folks."

The Associated Press happened to be there. I didn't know they were there, but they picked it up, released it, and the story went all over the country that I said Jimmy Carter was my kind of folks.

He *is* my kind of folks. I pray for him by name often, and he's one of the most unforgettable people I've ever met.

Let me tell you about one of the most unforgettable things that has ever happened in my life.

One Sunday night I was walking out of church and Gene Triggs, an executive with Mississippi Chemical

Corp. and a real active Democrat and civic minded citizen, walked up to me and said, "Jerry, I want to tell you something confidential. You'll be the third person in this entire county that knows what I'm fixing to tell you.

"There's a possibility that President Carter is coming to Yazoo City to hold a town talk similar to the one he did in Clinton, Massachusetts earlier in his presidential service. The people have been here and looked at our facilities and very frankly weren't too impressed with them. But we're still hoping when they get back to Washington and make a report to the President, he'll tell them, 'We're going to Yazoo City.'

"Jerry, inasmuch as you're leaving to do some shows out in Oklahoma, I just wanted to tip you off. We've checked the date this meeting would be held and we called Tandy Rice in Nashville, and he said you'd be home the day the President will be here. We'll call you later on and let you know when it's official."

I took off real early the next morning and went into Oklahoma and did a show at Elk City. My phone rang at the hotel and the word came: "Jerry, Brother Jimmy Carter will visit Yazoo City."

Then it hit the news and everyone was aware that the President was coming.

When I got back home, the whole city of Yazoo was bubbling and boiling just like an Alka-Seltzer. Man, we were excited. It was one more thrilling event coming off in our town.

All of this really impressed me because the President was supposed to be asked questions. We said, "What kind of questions does the President want to be asked?"

They emphatically informed us that under no circumstances would there be any suggestions as to what he ought to be asked. "This is going to be a fair and square meeting exactly like the President says it's going to be. He's just going to stand up before a bunch of citizens of

Yazoo City, and they're going to ask questions and he's going to answer the questions. And he's not going to have any idea what he's going to be asked."

This impressed me. I really thought that was great.

Dan Lee was the man who represented the White House in setting up the meeting in Yazoo City. Mayor Floyd E. Johnson did an excellent job on being the leader of the town, making sure that all arrangements were made properly, working with Dan Lee.

The suggestion was made that the folks who wanted to get into the President's town talk would register and fill out a form published in the Yazoo Daily Herald. The names of those who registered—several thousand did so—were put in a big drum. The drum was turned and they drew out the names. The first 1,400 names were the people who could get in to see the President. This was a wonderful way to do it.

I got a call one night from Mr. Owen Cooper, who is the fine man with whom the President stayed in Yazoo City. He said, "I just got a call from Peter Lynch. He wants to get in touch with you, and I'll have him call you."

Peter Lynch is the young man representing the White House who was responsible for getting the crowd to the airport in our capital city of Jackson when the President landed. When I called him, he asked, "Would you be willing to help us get a crowd at the airport to meet the President?"

"I sure will."

I suggested I make promos for all the radio stations in Jackson, which I did.

The evening before the President was to arrive, the Yazoo City townfolk threw a big watermelon cutting and a pickin' and a singin' down on our triangle.

The people of Yazoo City own the old Main Street School which is located on a big triangle. It's an art

157

center. We had a big watermelon cutting for the press. I entertained the crowd and we had the high school choral group to sing. It was one of the highlights of the festivities.

I had also suggested to Peter Lynch that I get on a very popular television show, "Coffee With Judy," on channel 3 in Jackson, and be interviewed by Judy Denson.

She interviewed me about the President coming, and I was excited and told everybody to meet me at the air-port. And they did, brother! Twenty thousand folks showed up.

I got up on the platform and entertained the people for about thirty minutes, then the President landed, and everything worked out beautiful. I rushed back to Yazoo City to be present for an interview on television just be-fore the President was to come on the network.

One of the greatest thrills I've ever had in my life was right in the middle of the question-and-answer pe-riod. Kenneth Helton stood up and the President said, "Yes, sir, you have a question?"

"Mr. President, I manage the local Sunflower Food Store. I'd like for you to comment on what kind of relief can we give the middle income man tax-wise. I'm con-cerned about them. And, as Jerry Clower says, 'Some-body needs to shoot in amongst us. We need some relief.' "

The President said, "Jerry is here tonight. He's a fine entertainer, and I admire him very much."

Well, I got emotional. I thought I was going to cry because all of the people present in the high school gym started applauding and screaming.

When the applause died down—and you know ap-plause is just like a narcotic to an entertainer—I caught myself wanting to stand up and take a bow. I was be-ginning to get up, but I said to myself, "Jerry, you sit down. This is the Jimmy Carter Show. You ain't on this show. What do you mean standing up?"

Then the President said, "Yazoo City is to be commended for a man like Jerry Clower living in Yazoo City."

Well, the people applauded again. When it died down again, the President said, "Jerry met me at the airport when I landed in Jackson a while ago. It was raining and he held my raincoat for me." Then he went on and answered the man's question.

Yes, this has to be one of the most unforgettable events in my life—President Jimmy Carter coming into my hometown, Yazoo City, and everything being run in such a beautiful manner.

I was most impressed with Carol Ann Rambo. She was in charge of all the press that accompanied the President to Yazoo City—and there was a whole drove of press folks.

The only thing that the people in Yazoo City were disappointed in was the last statement made by Sam Donaldson on ABC network television. I thought he took a cheap shot at the people of Yazoo City.

Yazoo City floated a bond issue and it passed by 80 percent to build a brand new beautiful high school. And the President of the United States in his opening remarks had commended the race relations of Yazoo City for passing that bond issue to build a new school where our children would have decent educational facilities. My own children go to the public schools. We are so thrilled about the progress we've been making.

And Sam Donaldson had the gall to take a cheap shot when he signed off the network television by saying, "Nineteen people asked questions here this evening. Sixteen were white. Three were black. This Yazoo City has a long way to go."

Well, now, had they let us select the folks who were

159

going to ask questions, we would have picked half white and half black. We've got that much sense—to where those do-gooders on the network wouldn't be criticizing us. But, inasmuch as anyone who wanted to stand up and ask a question could ask a question, the fact that just three blacks asked questions wasn't our fault. Sam Donaldson took a cheap shot at us, and I resent it.

One of the finest men God ever made, Owen Cooper, wrote Sam Donaldson and ABC a letter protesting this type of reporting. I still don't think that remark was called for, and I didn't like it.

The other side of it is that I'm a Christian and I'm willing to see Sam Donaldson's side.

My friend, Roy Blount, Jr., who is a very fine writer and who did the story on me in *Sports Illustrated* in 1973, and a very fine reporter, William Thomas, one of the top people with the Memphis *Commercial Appeal*, and a photographer with the *Commercial Appeal*, were all sitting in my den watching the playback with me. The minute Sam Donaldson made this statement, the photographer yelled, "That's a cheap shot."

Roy Blount, Jr. said, "I don't think he meant it like you think he means it. He wasn't criticizing the people of Yazoo City for just three blacks asking the questions. He was merely pointing out that we have a long way to go before blacks will take the initiative to ask more questions and to get more involved in public affairs."

If the man meant it the way Roy Blount, Jr. thought he meant it, fine. But I thought it was uncalled for. Until Sam Donaldson makes some kind of explanation about what he meant, I'm going to believe he was trying to be ugly and show us up as being bad folks when we are not bad folks. We have made more progress in race relations in Yazoo City than the hometown from where Sam Donaldson makes his big reports.

So, all in all, the President's visit that day to Yazoo

City was a beautiful thing for our town. We were thrilled that he came to see us.

The Owen Coopers—the people with whom President Carter spent the night—put the frosting on the cake when they announced that each and every individual who wanted to pass through their house and see the bed that the President had slept in, could come through it. Literally hundreds of people lined up for blocks the next afternoon after the President had gone and went through the Cooper home. That shows the beautiful all-out whole community effort that made this one of the most fantastic things that has ever happened in my lifetime.

The people told me how thrilled they were when the folks who came here with the President—Dan Lee and Carol Ann Rambo—remarked about how beautiful it was.

And I got thank-you notes. Dan Lee wrote me a note on White House stationery, thanking me for participating.

It was just beautiful, and we'll never be the same again in Yazoo City.

My career has thrown me into the midst of record magnates, and corporation empire directors in the record business and publishing, and big network people. Also, I've been with some of the biggest ad agencies and biggest executives in the nation. I'm very much impressed by some of these fantastically talented people.

But let me tell you about the most unforgettable company I've ever met: Mississippi Chemical Corporation.

Back in the late '40s, the Farm Bureau of Mississippi sponsored a meeting in our capital city, Jackson, and the president of the bureau got up and said, "Ladies and gentlemen, what is the most prevalent problem among farmers today?"

Without a doubt, the decision was reached that the most prevalent problem among farmers at that time was the scarcity of, or inability to buy, nitrogen fertilizers.

We've got to have nitrogen fertilizers in order to make a crop. So committees were appointed, and they met with the major manufacturers to see if there was any way to get nitrogen, especially at a little fairer price. They even talked about methods of substitutes or how to get more nitrogen from someplace else.

While walking out of one of those meetings, a young man named Owen Cooper looked over at a friend and said, "We ought to build us a plant—the farmers ought to build their own nitrogen plant."

"Ha ha ha," people laughed. "Owen, you couldn't get farmers that organized to build their own nitrogen plant."

Owen Cooper went before the state legislature of Mississippi and asked them to appropriate $50,000 with the money used to poll farmers in a few counties. Simply make a questionnaire asking, "If you could invest some money in your own nitrogen plant that would insure you of getting your nitrogen every year, would you be interested?"

About 80 percent of those returning the questionnaire answered: "Yes, we would."

This man, Owen Cooper, had a dream. He put legs to that dream. And sweat and hard work. He hired a few key people. Some of these people were semi-retired or about to retire—they were versed in agriculture and they took a job as field representative, which simply meant they would sell stock in the company. This cut out the big load charge. They sold this stock for a modest salary and expenses. They hit the highways and the hedges, calling on farmers, and asking, "Sir, how many tons of ammonia nitrate do you need?"

"I use ten tons a year."

"All right, sir, it would take a $75 investment in this company to get one ton of ammonia nitrate. It would take about that much money to build that much of this plant."

Farmers from all over the Mid-South invested money in Mississippi Chemical Corporation. The biggest newspapers in the state of Mississippi editorially fought it, said it was a bad scheme. The governor of Mississippi at that time said, "It will not work." However, to his eternal credit, when it was a fantastic success, the governor admitted it, visited the plant, and said he was proud of the people who put it together.

Mississippi Chemical Corporation decided to locate in Yazoo City. Had a farmer invested $100 the year they started making fertilizer—this was in 1952—and owned that $100 worth of stock and used the ammonia nitrate allocated on the stock, his return would have been up to the year 1975: $966.88.

Do you hear me? Isn't that beautiful? Mississippi Chemical Corporation is the first farmer–owned synthetic nitrogen plant ever constructed anywhere in the world. It's one of the most complete plant food companies in the world. Some of the plants are the largest in the world. And for twenty-one out of the twenty-five years, the plant food was bought for less from Mississippi Chemical than any other manufacturer.

My soul, what a fantastic success! And the $100 original investment can be sold today for $500. Mississippi Chemical Corporation through this date in 1977 has paid $275,000,000 in cash back to its stockholders. The assets of the company today are in excess of $350,000,000.

Yes, Mississippi Chemical Corporation is a fantastic

corporation. It was, and is, run by fantastic people—
its executives are tops in their field. Mississippi Chemical
is going full blast today. It's a company with a heart and
is one of the most unforgettable things I've ever known
about. Beautiful.

One of the most unforgettable events that I've ever
known took place back in September 1969 when the
Yazoo City Indians played the Murrah Mustangs of
Jackson.

I had been down in Florida on a business trip selling
fertilizer for Mississippi Chemical Corp. I landed back
in Jackson and went by Primos Country Kitchen about
one o'clock. The special for the day was corned beef
and cabbage.

Apparently they figured all the lunch guests were
through eating because when they brought me my corned
beef and cabbage, it was a great big platter full. I ate up
on it with some cornbread and some good cool butter-
milk, and I was feeling good.

But for about the last two days I had been noticing a
soreness in the left side of my stomach. I just knew I had
pulled a muscle in it.

Halfway to Yazoo City driving up that highway, with
those beautiful kudzu vines and rolling hills, the left side
of my old belly got to hurting mighty bad.

So I pulled into the Yazoo City Hospital and asked
if Dr. John Chapman was making his rounds—and they
said he was. I went around to the emergency room and
the nurse told Dr. Chapman I needed to see him.

He came walking in and popped a thermometer in my
mouth and said, "Big man, you got a hot spot down
there, let's take your temperature. Sounds like to me,
based on what you said, you got diverticulitis."

As I look back on this, I thank God for a good doctor, because not long after that I met a fellow at a convention down in Alabama and he was out on the road traveling when he started hurting. He stopped off at a big medical center and they took out his appendix and sent him home. He was eaten up with diverticulitis, and he liked to have died.

But here was a doctor in a town of 12,000 that said, "Big man, it sounds like you've got diverticulitis. But we won't assume that's exactly what it is. There are some simple tests we can put you through and we'll know what you've got. But you've got to be put in the hospital. You go home and get your pajamas and come back."

"No, sir, Doctor Chapman, you're mistaken. This is Thursday and tomorrow is Friday, and tomorrow night Yazoo City High School is going to play Murrah in Jackson. Murrah's the number one rated football team by every poll, AP, UPI, and everybody in the state of Mississippi. Yazoo City is rated number two, and whoever wins that game is going to be number one in the whole state. My boy is playing—he plays offense and defense and also does the kicking and the punting. And I'm going to be there."

"Jerry, you aren't going home to get your pajamas; you're going in the hospital bed right now. You aren't even going to leave the hospital. Man, you've got a high temperature, and whatever that is in your belly is hot—and you're going to have to stay here in the hospital."

I boiled up.

"Nurse, get him a room."

It almost killed me, and he saw how dejected I was. "Jerry, if I get your temperature down, tomorrow evening when it comes time for your wife Homerline to leave to go to Jackson to see the Yazoo City Indians play Murrah, I'll let you just go out of the hospital. You can't check out, but you can go get in the car, go down there and watch the game, and come back and go back into the hospital."

"All right."

He put me in that hospital and they commenced to take those tests and giving me the pills. About two o'clock the next afternoon—Friday—Dr. Chapman walked back in my room.

"Big man, I'm sorry, but you can't go anywhere. That belly is still hot, your temperature is still high, and you aren't going to be able to see the game."

It about killed me. One of the reasons it bothered me not to get to go to the game was that I had been asked by Coach Sammy Howard before each and every football game for several years to come into the dressing room and, just before the boys ran out for the kickoff, to lead the team in prayer. I looked forward to doing that, did it for thirty straight games and only missed this one time.

Homerline brought me my radio. I turned it on and found out that big Murrah dressed out over eighty-five people and little old Yazoo City had thirty-four. They kicked off to us and Larry Kramer, our great running back, took that ball on the goal line. The announcer said, "He's breaking loose! Ray Clower makes the final block at the fifty yard line, and Larry Kramer's gone for a touchdown! The score is six to nothing."

Man, did I get excited. About eight nurses came running into my room. "Mr. Clower, you've got to be quiet. You can't scream and holler. You'll disturb this whole hospital. We'll have to take this radio away from you."

It would have taken an army to have done that.

But I turned it down a little, calmed myself, and got me a pad and started keeping notes. And Yazoo City beat Murrah that night 20 to 6.

Why is that one of the most unforgettable events of my life? I'll tell you why.

The next morning, there was a knock on my door in that hospital. I said, "Come in."

And the entire squad of the Yazoo City Indians walked into my room and gave me the game ball. As I sit here writing this book, I see that game ball prominently displayed among my most valuable treasured gifts that people have presented to me through the years.

Yes, the Yazoo City—Murrah football game, September 1969, is one of the most unforgettable events of my life.

By the way, the next time the polls came out, number one in the state was Yazoo City. And those little scrapping boys went on undefeated the rest of the year and were the champions of Mississippi.

16

Stories from the South

One of the finest couples I've ever known in my life—
Aunt Penny and Uncle Jesse—lived near us. When I
was a young'un, if folks got old and they were respected,
people called them aunt and uncle.

They were fine godly folk, but Aunt Penny upset us
boys some kind of bad because she was just too optimis-
tic. I don't care what happened, she'd always say, "It
could be worse."

I mean when the Japanese bombed Pearl Harbor, well,
"It could have been a lot worse."

Your milk cow died. "It could have been a lot worse."

The mail rider ran over a frying size chicken just
before Sunday dinner. She'd say, "Well, it could have
been a lot worse."

So us boys decided we'd trick her. We went up there
the middle of one afternoon and told her that her husband, Uncle Jesse, wasn't coming home that night, that

the devil had got him and toted him off. Aunt Penny said it could have been a lot worse.

My brother Sonny said, "My goodness, woman. *How?*"

"Well, the devil could have made poor old Jesse tote him."

A doctor friend of mine told me that he needed a plumber mighty bad. He called for a plumber and finally got one after three weeks.

The plumber came during the Christmas holidays and unclogged all of the pipes in ten minutes. The water was running and everything was fine.

"Mr. Plumber, don't send me a bill," the doctor said. "Tell me, how much do I owe you?"

"Seventy-five dollars."

"Seventy-five dollars? Why you haven't worked ten minutes. I'm a doctor and I don't make that kind of money."

"When I was a doctor, *I* didn't make that kind of money either," answered the plumber.

This farmer was sitting out in the backyard discussing with his manager about buying a new bull. It was imperative that they had to bring some more bloodlines onto the farm.

There were three bulls already on the place, and they were out in the lot, and they could hear this guy talking.

The first bull said, "Looka hear, I've been here three years, and there ain't but fifty cows here. Thirty of them cows belong to me. And I don't care what kind of

Mr. Bigshot Bull he brings here, I ain't about to be nice to him."

The second bull said, "I ain't been here but a year and a half, but I agree with you, I ain't about to put up with it. We'll make life miserable for him. I guarantee you, I ain't about to share nothing with him."

The third bull said, "I ain't been here but six months. And I don't have but about five cows that even like me. But I'll tell you right now I ain't giving up them five. Mr. Bull is going to be in a bad state of affairs."

The next day here came one of those big long trucks. Drove up in the yard. Let down the end gate. And walking off that thing came the biggest, raunchiest looking old Brahma bull ever been. It weighed way over a ton. It was snorting.

The bull didn't have to look through the fence to see the cows grazing down in the pasture. He flatfooted just looked over the fence.

There was a great big hump on his back. He went strutting around the lot. Man, he was something!

The first bull said, "You know, I've been doing a little thinking; it was real ugly for me to have the attitude that I've been having. I just think I'll share with him."

The second bull said, "You know, I've changed my mind, too. I want to do the right thing about it."

The third bull busted out of the stall, ran out in the lot, commenced to pawing the ground, bristles up on his back as he was trotting around out there. Pawing the dirt and bellowing.

The bulls said, "Hey, man, what in the world are you doing? Are you crazy? That thing will kill you."

He said, "Look, I just want to make for sure that he knows that I'm a bull."

LET THE HAMMER DOWN!

One of the reasons I wanted to transfer from Southwest Mississippi Junior College to Mississippi State to play football in the Southeastern Conference was because Mississippi State played Baylor University, that good Baptist school in the Southwest Conference.

When I was signed to a scholarship at Mississippi State, I called my mama long distance and said, "Mama, just think, your poor little old country boy is going to play against the largest Baptist university in the world."

I got ready for them people. I didn't miss prayer meeting for a whole year. I got ready for them. I knew they were the same kind of Baptists I was.

When we got ready to play Baylor, I got the scouting report and I looked down hurriedly to see who the man was that I was going to play in front of. Do you know what the report said about a guard named Rayfield? Big, aggressive, tough, likes to play it mean. In fact when he was ordained as a Baptist preacher, he had two black eyes.

We played Baylor in Memphis that year. That quarterback was chunking that football to a fellow named Isbell. The coach sent word, "Jerry, that quarterback's got too much time to throw the ball. You get to him and get to him quick."

I rushed back in there and with every fiber of my being I reached for him, and I was just before getting my hands on him and that preacher Rayfield forearmed me back of my head. Shoved my face down in that dirt and in that grass. My bottom lip and bottom teeth scooped up a big mouthful of that dirt like a dragline.

I jumped up spitting and knocking the grass and dirt out of my mouth. "Fellow, you're the dirtiest thing I ever played against in all my life. And you're supposed to be a Baptist preacher playing for Baylor."

And he stood up erect. They had done throwed the ball for a touchdown. He put his hand over his heart

and he pointed his long finger right in my face. "The Bible says the meek shall inherit the earth."
And I had just inherited a mouth plumb full of it.

Kirk Garner was a very religious fellow. He was in church every time those church doors opened.

One day he walked out on the front porch, and an airplane had just finished doing some skywriting. He didn't know an airplane could do that.

The airplane was gone, and the words that the plane wrote were fading out. Kirk stood on the front porch and looked at it. He broke and ran back in the house and told his wife, "Callie, it's judgment. God's done wrote it in the sky."

"Kirk, I don't hear no horns blowing or bells ringing. I don't believe it's judgment."

It aggravated Kirk to the extent that he ran, jumped off the front porch, tripped, and fell over the faucet he had driven into the ground to make folks think he had running water. Actually, Kirk toted water a mile and a half from a branch back behind his house. A great big antenna stretched across the roof, and Kirk didn't even have a radio.

He hit that dirt road and he started running toward my daddy's house. He was kicking up dirt; he was scared to death that judgment was there.

Mr. Halley, a man down the road, saw him coming and knew something bad was wrong with Kirk running that fast, kicking up that dust, so he got out in the middle of the road and bearhugged him when he came by to stop him.

"Slow down, Kirk. What in the world's happening?"
"Mr. Halley, it's judgment."
"Why would you say that?"

"I saw it wrote in the sky. God's done wrote it up there. Judgment."

"Kirk, that's Pepsi-Cola."

"Sir?"

"That's Pepsi-Cola, Kirk. An airplane wrote that up there and the airplane has been gone five minutes, and you just saw that writing."

"Oh, Mr. Halley, you know that ain't no Pepsi-Cola."

"Yes, it is. The airplane wrote it and it has done gone. So you just calm down. It ain't judgment."

The next morning Kirk came down to my daddy's house, and they were standing out in the back yard. Kirk was telling my papa this story. Daddy asked him, "What would you have done had it been judgment?"

"I was just going to keep running until judgment overtook me."

17

The Hustlers

One of the most prevalent questions I'm asked at news conferences and when I travel is, "Jerry, how can you be successful? What is success?"

Unfortunately, most people judge success by how much money you've got and what you're worth. That ain't necessarily so.

Regardless of your occupation, whether you drive a truck, dig a ditch, milk a cow, sweep a street, or haul garbage, if you're doing that job to the best of your ability, then you are successful. If you're loafing, if you're not giving an honest day's work for an honest day's pay, then you ain't successful. It's just that simple.

There are a lot of good people working in the fields today or doing other jobs, who are more successful than people who have a lot of wealth because maybe those people didn't apply themselves to the best of their ability. But if you are letting the hammer down and you're doing the best you can with what you've got, and you're doing it right, then, whatever you're doing, you are successful.

"What is one of the ways you can be a successful salesman?" people ask me. Now that's the thing I did more than anything else in my life.

I got out of Mississippi State University in January of 1951 and took a job the following March 1 as the assistant county agent at Oxford, Mississippi. I kept that job for a year; then I went commercial and started selling seed corn for Pfister Associated Growers. I moved to Clarksdale, Mississippi, and lived there in 1952 and 1953. My son Ray was born in Clarksdale. After two years of selling seed corn, I had the privilege of going to work for Mississippi Chemical Corporation on March 1, 1954. And I've been associated with that company ever since.

But if you ask me the question, "How can you be a successful salesman?" or "How can you be a success in your vocation?" . . . well, back when I was a full–time salesman, they used to get some learned folks to come and hold conferences. They'd have a sales meeting and some big, world–renowned fellow would come and show us how to do a better job of selling. Some of the things he recommended for us to do, I didn't have sense enough to do.

It gets back to my pet peeve of taking simple things and making them complicated. But in my over twenty years of being a salesman in agri–business, I'd like to list three things that I feel an individual can do to become more successful in the vocation that he or she is in. Anybody can apply these three things to make you more successful, regardless of what you're doing.

Number one. Be courteous.

Anybody can be courteous. There's nothing that bothers me any more than for me to go into a public place to try to buy something and somebody in there is not courteous to me.

Years ago an elderly fellow went by an Eastern university, an Ivy League university, and said he'd like. to have an audience with the president. They told him that the president was busy that morning. He said, "I sure would like to see him, and I'll wait."

In a little while that president came out and said, "You can have three minutes; state your business." The president wasn't too courteous to this old gentleman.

"Well, sir, I don't mind you being busy and being tied up, but you don't have to come out here and be discourteous to me. You know, I was just thinking whether I ought to build me a university similar to the great university you've got here, or whether I ought to give you and your university a hundred million dollars."

Well, people, Mr. Leland C. Stanford went to California and he built Stanford University. It's a fine university. Once I had the opportunity to go on a tour of that beautiful facility. In one of the buildings, I remarked, "That sure is a beautiful overhead up there. My, how pretty that is."

The guide showing me around said, "Mr. Clower, Mr. Stanford was in the gold mining business and he wanted that ceiling to be pretty, so he put gold leaf up there."

Yes, it pays to be courteous!

Number two. Hustle.

People will respect a man or woman who is not lazy.

I buy insurance from a man, not from a company. I buy from this man because he's a hustler. Man, he gets it on! He's going to make so many calls a day. He's disciplined. He believes in working and earning his living by the sweat of his brow. And I respect him for that.

A few years ago, I took my son Ray to see the St. Louis Cardinals play baseball. As luck would have it, that was the day they were unveiling the statue of the great Stan

Musial. I was thrilled that my son would be able to participate in this momentous occasion.

To recognize the great Stan Musial, the Cardinal organization had invited back to St. Louis all of the players who were on the 1941 Cardinal team when Musial broke in as a rookie.

Harry Caray, the announcer for the St. Louis Cardinals, went to the pitcher's mound with a microphone, and he announced to a standing–room–only crowd: "Ladies and gentlemen, we're going to introduce these players one by one before the start of this ball game, and let you see these oldtimers who were playing back in 1941 when Stan Musial broke in as a rookie."

Caray introduced the first one. "Batting number one and playing center field, Terry Moore."

The fans gave a nice round of applause for Terry Moore, who walked to center field with a slight limp.

"And now, batting number two and going to shortstop, Marty Marion."

He got a nice round of applause as he walked out to shortstop.

"Now, batting number three—"

Folks started getting up all over them stands. They started screaming. They yelled and hollered and whooped and stomped. And I couldn't get over it. I didn't know what was happening. Ray and I were sitting there and everybody was going wild. So I got up with them. With the thunderous applause and folks screaming, you couldn't hear anything.

Harry Caray, the announcer, hushed up. I told this old man standing by me, "Look, these people have lost their mind. Stan Musial isn't coming out now because he batted fourth and played right field."

The old fellow standing next to me was so excited that he threw his Coke straight up in the air. He threw it all over everybody and yelled, "But, son, you don't understand. The Old Hustler is fixing to come out. Man, the fellow is fixing to come out that believed in giving an honest day's work for an honest day's pay. He hustled. Why, I remember seeing him score from first base once on a bunt."

When the crowd finally hushed up and sat back down, Caray continued, "And now, batting number three and going to left field, Country Boy Enos Slaughter!"

Folks, here comes Enos Slaughter with a business suit on, with that bald head, a'coming out of the dugout with his head thrown back, and he ran wide open to left field. They gave him another standing ovation.

I sat my son down and told him, "Ray, let daddy teach you a lesson right here. Here is a man that's remembered because he wasn't lazy. He hustled!"

St. Louis still remembers the old Country Boy, Enos Slaughter.

Hustle!

Number three. Be yourself!

Not only should an individual be courteous and hustle, but at all times be himself or herself.

Many salesmen are a lot better salesmen than their district manager, but they're mocking him. A lot of individuals in vocations other than selling would do a lot better job if they didn't mock or mimic some of the people who were bossing them.

Be yourself.

Occasionally, some of my preacher buddies mock Billy Graham. Every time they mock Billy Graham, they fall flat on their face because God didn't make but one Billy Graham. I wish he'd make a few more. I wish he'd raise up a black Billy Graham. That's what I wish. How beautiful that would be.

Be yourself. When I was growing up at Route 4, Liberty, the Lord called a young man to preach. He went off to college to study how to be a preacher and had been gone from the East Fork Community of Route 4 for about six months. He had been off studying, and he came home for Christmas holidays.

The pastor of our little East Fork Baptist Church thought it would be the polite thing to do to invite this young man to preach one Sunday morning.

That young fellow, who had been gone just six months, got up in the pulpit and you would have thought he was born in Scotland. You could hardly understand what he was saying.

He didn't say "God" any more. He rolled it around and said it, "Gaw-dah!" He screwched up his mouth, puckered up his lips.

He didn't say "morning." He said "mawninginging" and let the "ing" just ring across the auditorium of the little church.

"I ain't gonna listen to him," my brother Sonny said.

"Sonny, hush; you're disturbing the morning worship service," I told him.

Sonny rammed fingers in both of his ears. "I ain't gonna listen; I ain't gonna listen to nothing he's saying."

"Why?"

"Jerry, he ain't being himself. And I don't respect a fellow that don't try to be what he is. I just don't respect him for being something he ain't. He growed up right here with us and he ought to talk like we talk, and he ought to do things like we do. He's not being himself. He thinks he's better than us."

My brother Sonny thought about it some more. "What makes me so cottonpickin' mad about the whole deal is that he was just as poor as us when he was growing up. In fact, one summer him and his folks was poorer than we was. Jerry, don't you remember the summer that they was so poor that that boy's mama fed him so many turnip greens she had to keep a coal oil rag tied around his ankles to keep the cut worms from getting him?"

Be yourself.

The Bible says to honor your father and mother. Do it!

I was in school with some people who were ashamed of their parents, ashamed of where they came from. My soul, this will never work.

While playing football at Mississippi State University, there was a guy on the team who kept popping off about what all his folks had, how great they were, everything was fine, he came from a big home, and he had ritzy this and ritzy that.

One day an old country man showed up on the campus looking for his boy. This boy wouldn't have anything to do with his daddy. He didn't want anybody to know that that was his papa.

About six months later, we were having skull practice over at the athletic dormitory. All of the football team was sitting around watching the coach explain plays on the blackboard.

An old gentleman was fumbling at the door. It was a glass door and you could see through it. Obviously, he was looking for a place but didn't know where he was. He opened the door and stepped into the room.

This wrinkled old man, very poorly dressed, was embarrassed. He had walked into the wrong meeting room.

But my buddy Pete, a big guard weighing 240 pounds and standing six feet two inches tall, stood up. "My soul, coach, excuse me just for a minute. This is my daddy, and I want to introduce him to all of my teammates."

He went up there and put his arm around that old man and kissed him right in front of the football team.

And I thought: *my soul, who had you rather have blocking for you? Pete? Or that cat who didn't want to recognize his old daddy?*

You want to get ahead in the world? You want to be successful? Be courteous. Hustle. And be yourself.

I highly recommend it to you.

18

The End

Well, how do you like that? I bet a lot of my college and high school teachers would be surprised that I'm now wrapping up my second book. The first one kind of caught most of them off guard.

I started to title this book *Things I Meant to Say in My First Book*. Because even before my first book came out I was thinking about more things to put in it.

I had forgotten to mention my daughter-in-law Nan. But time takes care of everything—and, Nan, I count it a privilege to mention you, as you are my daughter-in-law and I love you.

And I now get to correct the only mistake I've been able to find in the first book. Somehow, Point Clear, Alabama came out Point Cedar, Alabama in *Ain't God Good!* Let me make it perfectly clear, it's Point Clear!

Thanks so much for your letters informing me about the effect that the book had on your lives. Beautiful! I hope you enjoyed this one, too.

LET THE HAMMER DOWN!

Life keeps getting better, and the stories keep coming. Who knows? Gerry Wood and I just might sit down again and come up with another book.

Ain't God Good? You bet!

You know why? Because he lets the hammer down.

You, too, can let the hammer down. Join me, friend, and we'll let that hammer down together.

Discography

Since I'm asked questions all the time from fans across the country—"Jerry, which one of your albums has the coon hunt on it, or talks about Ol' Highball, or which one talks about how your mama makes biscuits?"—I have asked the publishers of this book to list a complete glossary and rundown on all the albums I have ever made and the stories contained on each album.

Some of you may think this is commercial and that I'm just doing this to sell albums. That's part of it. But the main reason I'm doing this, seriously, is to render a service.

So here it is, folks. All of my works available on albums, 8-track tapes or cassettes. Love you. Jerry.

JERRY CLOWER FROM YAZOO CITY MISSISSIPPI TALKIN'
MCA 33 (selections previously released on Decca album DL7-5286)
Introduction by Big Ed Wilkes
A Coon Huntin' Story

LET THE HAMMER DOWN!

Bully Has Done Flung a Cravin' on Me
Baby Goes to College
Homecomin' Steaks!
The Graduate Returns
Marcel's Talkin' Chain Saw
The Chauffeur and the Professor
Good Citizenship

MOUTH OF MISSISSIPPI
MCA 47 (selections previously released on Decca album
    DL7-5342)
Knock Him Out, John
Public School Music Class
The Rat Killin'
Pistol Pete
Those Tigers Are Bad, Wet or Dry
Clower Takes a Trip
Judgment in the Sky
Green Persimmon Wine
Ole Highball
The Meek Shall Inherit the Earth
New–Gene Ledbetter
The Last Piece of Chicken
A Double Fire Place
Little Red

CLOWER POWER
MCA 317
Second Down and Goal to Go
Ole Brumey Wasn't Runnin' a Coon
The Public School Music Class Learns a Song
I'm That Country
Marcel Says No School Today
Peanut Boilin' Was Required
Life at Route Four—Liberty Mississippi
How to Back into Show Business
Three Footballs in a Game Ain't Fair
All about Clovis Ledbetter
Marcel Wins a Bet

186

The Ole Timey Ice Box
Uncle Virsi Ledbetter
Brother Sonny Goes to Church
My Mama Made Biscuits
The Flying Jenny
King Solomon Said
Signaling for a Fair Catch
Little Katy Learns a Lesson
What Christmas Means to Me

COUNTRY HAM
MCA 417
The She Coon of Women's Lib
Panama Limited
The Time We Played Clemson
Marcel Is in Trouble
Mr. Duval Scott
Home in the Country
U.S. Exports
Ole Slantface
The New Fad
My Pet Peeve
Marcel's Invasion
The Young People of Today
All Right
A New Bull
In High Cotton
Be Yourself

LIVE IN PICAYUNE
MCA 486
Live in Picayune
Physical Examination
The Plumber
Bird Huntin' at Uncle Virsi's
Marcel's Snuff
The Tarzan Movie
Rattlesnake Roundup
Aunt Penny Douglas

LET THE HAMMER DOWN!

A Box for Clovis
Marcel Ledbetter Moving Company
The Coon Huntin' Monkey
Marcel's Old Goose
Uncle Virsi's Horse
The Chain
Marcel's Hair Growing Secret
Hot Apple Pie
Soppin' Molasses
New–Gene's 4–H Trip
What's His Number
Counterfeiters
You're Fixin' to Mess Up

THE AMBASSADOR OF GOODWILL
MCA 2205
Titus Plummeritis
Writing in My Bible
Warm Water Heater
Tough Nut
Clovis and Beck
The Wise Men
Dig a Dug Well
Marcel Goes Quail Huntin'
It Coulda Been a Lot Worse
Wanna Buy a Possum?
The Headless Man
Flying to the Opry
A Nickel's Worth of Cheese
Marcel's Brother Goes to Jail
Runnin' the Coon
Uncle Virsi Sees the Ocean
Mr. Jake Ledbetter
The Clumsy Mule
The Pet Squirrel
The House I Live In

AIN'T GOD GOOD! (A LAY PREACHING SERMON BY JERRY CLOWER)
Word Records WST-8737

Ain't God Good!
Ain't God Good! (concluded)

ON THE ROAD
MCA 2281
Airport Goodbyes
The Hot Hotel
Uncle Virsi's Trial
Rats in the Corn Crib
Clovis Gets a Job
Mr. Duvall Scott's Chicken
Steel Marbles
Tar Baby
Deep Water Baptist
Stealing Teacakes
My First Banana
Hitler on the Front Porch
Fifteen Yard Penalty
Cutworm Smith
New-Gene and the Lion
My Katy Burns